Winning the War
WITHIN

A Biblical Strategy
for Spiritual Warfare

Jay E. Adams

TIMELESS TEXTS
Woodruff, SC

Recommended Dewey Decimal Classification: 248.4
Recommended Library of Congress Classification: BV4501.2.A287
Suggested Subject Headings: 1. Christian life 2. Spiritual life.

ISBN: 0-89081-732-4 old number
ISBN: 1-889032-00-X new number
Printed in the United States of America

CONTENTS

You Are at War!

1. Who Started It? 11

2. The War Within 19

3. How You Got Involved 23

4. What's the War Like? 31

5. Some Cases in Point 41

6. The Enemy's Power 51

7. The Enemy Within 59

8. Fighting with the Spirit's
   Sword 71

9. The Believer's Other Weapons 85

10. Calling In Reinforcements 93

11. Defeat 103

12. Hindrances 113

13. Maintaining a Military Mentality 127

14. Deserters 133

15. The Outcome 141

    Conclusion 149

    Notes

Winning the War
WITHIN

A Biblical Strategy
for Spiritual Warfare

You Are at War!

Christian, you are at war! You have been so since the day you were born. Indeed, you have served two different causes in two different armies radically opposed to each other.

These facts may astound you; you may even question or doubt the claim. Circumstances may seem to indicate otherwise—but it is true! God's Word, which cannot fail, says so.

When was the last sermon you heard, or book you read, about your duties as a soldier of Jesus Christ? Perhaps it's been so long ago that you have forgotten. When was the last time you sang "Onward Christian Soldiers" or "The Son of God Goes Forth to War"—or have these songs been eliminated from your hymnbook?

You may be one of the growing number of new converts to Christianity to whom nothing has *ever* been said about this war. In many circles today the fact of Christian warfare is so seldom mentioned, and therefore so little known, that many (perhaps most) believers are unaware of it.

One man, when asked about his part in the war, answered, "What war?" Another said, "What are you talking about? There's no war going on!"

Even ministers and seminarians seem surprised when I say in class, "The ministry is war." Pastors suddenly come alive to the fact, however, when I sometimes add, "...and many of the bullets come from behind!" Paul spoke of the ministry as "fighting the good fight," and he encouraged Timothy to "endure hardness as a good soldier of Jesus Christ." That was the New Testament emphasis.

Why has a significant segment of the church ignored or suppressed this all-too-important biblical truth? And what must be done about it? Those are two questions about which this book will have something to say. For now, all I need to say is that the same forces that have spawned an effete Christianity that shuns confrontation, glorifies self, and represents Jesus as a Savior who can add a dimension to your happiness (rather than one who will radically change your life) are at work. This cowardly self-indulgence of which I am speaking has been largely the result of doctrinal defection that fails to grapple with the hard truths of God's Word, or explains them away. At present it seems that the mentality of an overprosperous Christianity is very much like that of the first-century Judaism that rejected Christ because it wanted the crown without the cross.

Whatever the cause, it is clear that the church is asleep on the battlefield; she has laid down her arms unilaterally and has settled for an uneasy peace.

The war is being fought on a number of fronts. It has cosmic dimensions, hinted at in Daniel and other places and is fought on two levels in this earth. It is the battles at these two levels—one outward, the other inward—that are our responsibilities as members of the church. Every Christian, no matter how humble or simple, is involved in the war at both levels. While the outer battle is vital and pressing, it cannot be fought as it should be unless the Christian is successfully winning the war *within*. Therefore, because it is the more fundamental and foundational effort, this book is dedicated to exploring the biblically related problems and solutions having to do with the war at that level.

But the war within is fought invisibly in the depths of one's soul—where no one else can see or fully understand all its dimensions. It is a war that no Christian may escape and one that every Christian must fight. You are in a battle every day if you know Christ as your Savior. No one else can fight your battles for you.

Some of you are having trouble at home with your children or spouse. Perhaps the greatest battle you fight is over what to say to them—how to act and react to hostility, rebellion, or neglect. That is a battle you must fight *within*, and it may be one you are losing.

Perhaps you have a problem keeping a job. There is something about your anger and sharp tongue that leads sooner or later to your dismissal. And that same tongue has alienated friends and family as well. You may by now be dispirited, ready to give up. You have lost battles within so often that you wonder, "What's the use?" You may even be thinking of taking your life.

Sickness may have you down. The burden of caring for an aged parent may seem to be more than you can take. You are discouraged and defeated over your marriage. Or you may be tempted to commit adultery.

Whatever your problem, you may be sure that it has inner implications. No matter how great its outer aspects, the battle within always rages hotter. And, it is there—within your innermost being—that battles ultimately are won or lost.

Do you know how to fight the war within? Granted, there has been all too little teaching to show you how. Indeed, because of frequent setbacks, you may wonder whether there is a way to win.

This book—reflecting the spirit of the Word of God—has been written to tell you in no uncertain terms that *there is* a way to victory. And, avoiding the path of mere theory, it explains how *you*, no matter how many times you have been defeated in the past, can begin to *consistently* win the battles within.

Are you ready to learn? Then come with me to basic training, to a thorough study of what our Commander-in-Chief has to say.

It might be well for you to get out your Bible right now and follow along. We shall be digging in to see what God wants you to do and how He expects you to accomplish His will. You, along with many others, can win the war within!

— 1

Who Started It?

How did this war begin? Who is involved in it? What is it all about? *Who will win?* These, and dozens of similar questions, arise. In this chapter I shall try to answer some of the more basic ones.

Clearly all wars are begun by someone for some purpose, even if the motives and the particulars are at times difficult to sort out. In this case the origin of the war and the issues involved are perfectly clear. Anyone who reads the Bible sympathetically can understand.

When God created man, He placed him in the Garden, then told him to subdue the earth and to multiply and fill it (Genesis 1:28). These were the commands to *control* and to *occupy*, to pursue scientific and social activities. But there were also two immediate commands plainly intended as warnings. First, while Adam and Eve were given access to fruit from all other trees in the Garden for their nourishment and enjoyment, they were explicitly commanded not to eat from the tree of the knowledge of good and evil that grew in the midst of the Garden (Genesis 2:15-17). Second, they were strictly commanded to "cultivate and care for" the Garden itself (Genesis 2:15 Berkeley).

The translation "care for" does not quite do justice to the original word, which actually means "guard." It is the same word used in Genesis 3:24, where the cherubim are said to have guarded the entrance to Eden once Adam and Eve had been cast out. And it is the word that Cain used when asking "Am I my brother's keeper ['guardian']?" (Genesis 4:9). Adam and Eve were explicitly told not to eat of the centrally located tree of the knowledge of good and evil and were warned that the Garden needed protection from alien, harmful influences. That is the background of the war about which we are speaking.

Satan, the leader of the angels that fell (2 Peter 2:4) was the first to rebel against God and His government of the universe. Now, with the creation of man, he brought that rebellion to the newly formed earth, hoping to recruit the human race to his cause. As we know (to our sorrow, misery, and death), man succumbed to Satan's temptation, believing his lies, and fell.

How the war between God and Satan began, or exactly what happened to this powerful creature that he should turn against his Creator, we do not know. The Scriptures give us only the most meager hints. Two passages often (wrongly) interpreted as referring to the fall of Satan and his angels are Isaiah 14 and Ezekiel 28. Though they certainly describe rebellion against God at its worst, they do not describe Satan's fall, but the rebellion and overthrow of the willful kings of Babylon and Tyre, as Isaiah 14:4 and Ezekiel 28:1 make clear. Note especially how twice the king of Tyre is told, "You are only human" (Ezekiel 28:2,9 Berkeley).

As to the war on earth, then, we know only that it was brought into the human sphere from the outside as part of a cosmic war between God and Satan that had been going on previously. The war on earth is but one front of the war of the heavens, and what happens in human history is but an aspect of what is transpiring in cosmic history. (Glimpses of these facts are seen in Revelation 12:7-9, Daniel chapters 11 and 12, and the Book of Job.)

War Declared on Earth!

But what happened in the Garden? Certainly it is unnecessary to recount here the story of man's seduction and fall, since it is an event well-known to every Bible-believing Christian. Yet the immediate consequence of the fall is not quite so well understood. Here is what the Scriptures say:

> Also I will put enmity between you and the woman; also between your offspring and her offspring [or seed]; He will crush your head and you will crush His heel (Genesis 3:15 Berkeley).

That passage is quite significant. In it war is declared, the antagonists are identified, and the outcome is assured.

God Himself, the Speaker in verse 15, was the One who declared war: "*I* will put enmity..." He said. So the war on earth was *God's* doing. This war declared by God included (as we shall see) all mankind. Every man, woman, or child, whether he knows it or not, is on one side or the other; he serves Satan or God—there is no neutrality. Jesus put it this way: "Whoever isn't with Me is against Me, and whoever doesn't gather with Me scatters" (Matthew 12:30). This means that *you* are either fighting for Christ or against Him.

You may not recognize the fact that you are scattering His work rather than gathering with Him, yet unless you have become a child of God—one of His seed—it is true. Everything you do, day by day, either helps or hinders His cause (that's what gathering and scattering mean); all those on the home front contribute to a war effort, even though they are not on the battlefield. Life for them may go on quite undisturbed at times, and they may forget all about the war. Nevertheless, they are contributing to the success (or failure) of the war by all that they do.

But what does the passage in Genesis 3:15 mean? Who is addressed? Who are the participants specifically singled out?

Symbolically, God destined the serpent to crawl on his belly in humiliation, licking or eating the dust (cf. Psalm 72:9; Micah 7:17), since he was the instrument by which Satan deceived humanity. But the key factors in the curse/promise passage quoted above are as follows:

The curse goes beyond the snake to the real culprit. It is *Satan* who is addressed in Genesis 3:15 when God uses the words "you" and "your." It is between the woman and Satan that God puts enmity (or declares war), and between their seeds. It is Satan who is to crush the heel of the woman's Seed as his own head is crushed beneath it. While this passage is certainly in the form of a judgment-curse upon Satan, it also contains a promise for the reader. In his effort to stamp out the Seed of the woman, the evil one will find that this very act is his own undoing. He bites the heel that is grinding his head into the ground.

This prophecy, often referred to as the "protevangelium" (the early preaching of the gospel), is ultimately a prediction of the cross. There Satan did his worst, thinking that he had defeated the One who had come to destroy his works (1 John 3:8). But by this very act Jesus, the Seed of the woman, was accomplishing His purpose. The cross was like the crushing of Christ's heel, because on the third day He rose in victory, and was like crushing Satan's head, because it was a fatal wound by which he is utterly defeated. Micah 5:2,3 and 1 Timothy 2:15 refer the prophecy of Genesis 3:15 to Christ.

However, there is more in the verse. Candlish says:

> Undoubtedly it is Christ who is principally pointed out; though at the same time, as the seed of the serpent may have a wider signification, denoting all his party among men (Matthew 3:7; John 8:41), so also the seed of the woman may be held to mean all who take part with the Lord, and are one with him in his holy war.[1]

Most commentators agree. Indeed, unless understood this way, the "seed" of the serpent has no referent. And it throws considerable light on the Old Testament when one reads this verse as an account of the war between the seeds, leading up to and culminating in the final battle between Satan and Christ, the Seed par excellence. The Scriptures teach that redeemed humanity, through Christ (with whom believers are identified), will have victory over Satan (cf. Romans 16:20). From the beginning to the end, Satan endeavored to cut off the line of Christ. At the outset, the godly line was represented by Abel and the line of Satan by Cain, who slew his brother. Referring to that event, John calls Cain the devil's seed when he says he "was of the evil one" (1 John 3:12). The destruction of the male children at the birth of Christ (Matthew 2:16) was a last-ditch effort to achieve the same end. Indeed, at every point between these events the history of Israel can be read as a war between the godly seed (chosen and placed by God in enemy territory to bring forth the Messiah)[2] and the world (the kingdom of Satan, his seed). On one occasion Jesus said:

> You are from your father the devil [i.e., his seed].... He was a murderer from the beginning, and didn't remain in the truth because the truth isn't in him (John 8:44).

But it is not about global war as such that this book is written. It is rather about the wars *within this war* that I am concerned. Satan has not only carried on his battles on a large scale, but he has been at work throughout the ages, and continues to carry on his nefarious activities now, as a defeated but vicious foe* seeking to destroy you *personally*. But take

---

* The word "Satan" means "The Adversary," a title given the devil that describes his general activity in the universe since he fell, and in particular his relationship to the godly seed of the woman (cf. 1 Peter 5:8: "*Your* opponent [adversary] the devil..."). Spurgeon once said: "There is something very comforting in the thought that the devil is an adversary.... I would sooner have him as an adversary than as a friend." From Tom Carter, compiler, *Spurgeon At His Best* (Grand Rapids: Baker, 1988), p. 57.

heart, Christian. God will not let you down. He is behind you all the way. And, as I shall show you in the pages to come, there is a way to win the war within. God has marshalled mighty forces and made them available to you. Through Christ you can be *more* than a conqueror!

2

The War Within

It would be a mistake to begin considering the war within before setting it in its larger context as a part of the global struggle initiated by God in the Garden. And it would be wrong to think of that struggle as the ultimate war, when in fact it is but a part—decisive as that part may be—of the greater war of the cosmos.

To focus on the war within apart from these contexts is to turn it into a personal conflict, a sort of feud between you and the devil. But while it is certainly personal, it is more than that. And because it is, the stakes are higher. You must always remember that the personal battles you fight are part of a larger whole in which the cause of Christ—not merely your own personal welfare—is on the line. That is why I took the time in the last chapter to make it clear that "the battle is the Lord's" (cf. 1 Samuel 17:47; 2 Chronicles 20:15). He declared it and He fights it—through you, and through millions of Christians like you all over the globe.

Same War

The war within is not a different war, then; it is the same one described in the previous chapter. In this inner war, the same antagonists are in view: Satan and his seed; the woman (representing Christ) and her seed (those who are in Christ). The goals, tactics, and weapons are also the same.

Therefore, what is said about one aspect of the war will often be helpful in describing and understanding another, at least to the extent to which commonalities hold. You will want to remember this as you notice our discussion moving from time to time from the smaller, inner war to the larger theater on which battles occur.

But though it is the same war, common in many respects, the battles fought in the soul of man each have their own peculiar elements, take on their own character, and call for special consideration, according to each individual involved. Moreover, from time to time the enemy shifts his point of attack and varies his tactics according to events transpiring in the global or cosmic theaters.

But the fact that the two wars are in reality but *one* war does not make the war within any less important. The war without is dependent on the war within. As battles are won or lost within the individual, so the overall war succeeds or fails. That is why it is so important to recognize the inner war as only one part of the larger campaign. Battles are won only as individuals fight valiantly on each chunk of battlefield turf. Wars are fought by individuals. And how they fight outwardly depends on their successes and failures in fighting within. So the importance of the inner war is obvious.

Yet Different

While the war within and the war without are linked, it is true that both the inner and outer wars of which the Bible speaks are quite different from those waged by earthly armies. When Paul wrote, "The weapons of our warfare are not carnal" (2 Corinthians 10:4 KJV), he was expressing something of that difference. When fighting the war without (to which Paul was referring in that passage), Christians must take up the armor of God, which in many respects is quite different from the armor of man. The reason why this is so is because—

1) God's kingdom is not of this world; otherwise His servants would fight as earthly armies do (cf. John 18:36).
2) The battle is the Lord's—and He wants that known;
3) God provides the weaponry, strategy, and strength;
4) The war without is in reality the *result* (and therefore the reflection) of the outcome of the war within, which itself is unique.

The war within is different still from the war without. It is fought on a more personal level. Like the war without, it involves the world, the flesh, and the devil, but as they seek to gain the victory over *you*. It has to do with *your* personal weaknesses, *your* sin, *your* misjudgments. That is why this book was written: to help you, as an individual, to take up God's arms, not only to defend yourself successfully against all the fiery darts of the devil, but also to help you take the battle to the enemy. Phillips Brooks put it this way:

Fight your battle for Him, with Him. So you shall fight it most persistently, most purely. Fight it with the sword bathed in heaven, and so you shall make it victorious, and grow strong and great yourself in fighting it.[1]

In turn, as you learn to do so, the war without will be advanced and the cosmic war will draw nearer to its full end.

3

How You Got Involved

Of course, you were born on the wrong side—that's why you had to be born again and become a member of the household of faith, a part of the seed of the woman. Until such a time as God regenerated you (gave you life to believe in Christ as your Savior), you scattered rather than gathered with Christ (Matthew 12:30b). You were in the grip of the evil one (1 John 5:19). Consequently, at that time, there was no war within.

But then came that wonderful day when you were taken captive in heart and soul by the Lord (2 Corinthians 10:5); you went over to His side. You were, in short, converted.

Sometimes new Christians are puzzled that things seem harder than before conversion. There are new problems in their marriage: John finds Mary's new interests foreign to his, separating them. There are new problems at work: Bob won't shade the truth to customers any longer. And there are new problems determining what is or is not in accord with God's will: Wholly new considerations come into play when making decisions. There is nothing unusual in this; indeed, it is to be expected. One of the main reasons for this change is that now there is a new element within, producing an internal struggle that could not have been experienced before.

Christians have found this to be true in one way or another. One woman whom we will call Sue tells her story:

> At age 18 years I married a very exciting and very atheistic young man. Not a Christian myself, I soon became an agnostic at best.
>
> Three years and two babies later I was confronted by a Christian to make a decision for Jesus Christ. This God allowed me to do. I then began to read the Word with great interest.
>
> My husband began noticing a change in me and hated it.
>
> He had from the beginning of our marriage stayed out late drinking, coming home with lipstick on his collar, etc. Five years and one more baby later...[after divorcing Sue] he left town with a woman and I later heard they had married.

Subsequently Sue remarried, this time to a Christian. But she began to have grave doubts as to whether her subsequent marriage was scriptural. Questions about whether she had committed adultery plagued her. She continues:

> We have been married 17 wonderful years. And yet I have been tormented by doubts about how we appeared in God's eyes. I would cry out to God..."If I'm an adulteress I'll leave my husband—anything to be in Your will."...so I have been at an impasse for around 12 years.

Then—I found your book (last Tuesday).
I've learned that I had been involved in an
unbeliever-separating-himself-from-a-be-
liever situation, and that this left me free. I
could also claim Matthew 19:9. I have been
properly divorced.

Here you can see two things at work. First, as I
suggested, when she became a Christian things got
worse. Her first husband hated her change and left
her. Then, second, five years into her second marriage her divorce and remarriage began to trouble
her when a pastor questioned the biblical validity of
those acts. Wanting to please God, she could not
merely go along as if nothing had happened.

So for the next 12 years she sought an answer and
was willing to take radical action to dissolve her
second marriage, if it was proved unbiblical. But,
unfortunately, until she happened upon my book
Marriage, Divorce and Remarriage in the Bible, she
could not find the help she sought, though she con-
sulted various sources.

But she never dropped the issue. Her concern led
her to read what she could find on the subject, and
ultimately to pick up the book mentioned above,
which in God's providence explained the scriptural
issues involved and brought peace to her mind.

With proper guidance Sue could doubtless have
been relieved much sooner. But she hung in there in
spite of it all, fighting and struggling until she was
able to win the victory. For His own reasons, God
was using this experience to strengthen Sue and
mold her for the days ahead. There would have been
no such agonizing battle, however (and no such
change of character as she evidenced), had she not

been converted. What gave the doubts their sharp edge was the possibility that she might be sinning against God. It is this kind of inner warfare that the Christian, and only the Christian, can experience.

Why is this so? What happens at conversion that brings this about? What is the nature of this struggle? Is it good? What must be done about it? This book attempts to answer all these questions, a couple of which the present chapter addresses.

What Happens at Conversion?

When the Lord Jesus Christ turns someone to Himself, He does so by changing his "heart." In the Scriptures, the word "heart" means something very different from its meaning in our Western cultures. Heart, for us, means emotions or feelings. In the Scriptures, heart means "the inner self, the decisions it makes and the interior life it leads." Heart is opposed not to the intellect (you'll find nothing in the Bible of the erroneous antithesis between intellect and emotion often expressed by preachers: "What we need is less head knowledge and more heart knowledge") but to the outer person (cf. such verses as Matthew 15:8; 1 Peter 3:4; 1 Samuel 16:7). Heart, in biblical thought, includes the whole inner person—intellect, emotion, and will. Its use often indicates what one *truly* is over against what he seems to be outwardly (cf. Romans 6:17: "from the heart"—i.e., sincerely, genuinely).

The unregenerate heart is unable to receive the things of God. Inwardly (i.e., truly) the unbeliever is not only ignorant of but resistant to the truth of God. All this is clear from 1 Corinthians 2:9-16. As I sit here this moment, there are sounds and sights all around me that I can neither hear nor see. But if I were to turn on the TV, I could pick them up. Paul says that the unsaved are like that: "Eye has not seen, ear has not heard" what God has prepared for His children. Why? They don't have the receiving set. When the Holy Spirit enters, He enables us to receive what God has prepared for those who love Him. In that passage the unbelieving heart is also said to be unable even to conceive of the things that God has prepared for those who love him (verse 9). In Ezekiel 36:26 his heart is called a heart of "stone." Stone is dead, resistant, cold.

But at conversion God gives a "new heart" of "flesh" (Ezekiel 36:26). This new heart is said to be like *flesh* in contrast to *stone* because it is alive to the things of God, it is receptive rather than resistant, and it is warm toward God and other people. In Romans 5:5 Paul put it this way:

> We need not be ashamed of hope because God's love has been poured into our hearts through the Holy Spirit Who was given to us.

The change, then, is twofold: 1) our capacity is changed (we acquire a new disposition so that we may love and learn the things of God), and 2) we have within us a new power upon which to draw (as the Holy Spirit takes up residence in our hearts, illuminating us and energizing us). For the first time, He enables us to love God and our neighbor in ways that please Him (Romans 8:8).

All this is wonderful, of course, but it does create new problems. The world outside does not understand the change (cf. 1 Corinthians 2:15b;

1 Peter 4:4) and often reacts negatively to it. That is perhaps the first noticeable result of beginning to live for Christ. But there is also the inner struggle itself to contend with.

The devil is not happy that you deserted him and went over to his enemy. (In Colossians 1:13 Paul describes conversion as a transfer of allegiances in which you have become a citizen of the kingdom of light, repudiating the dominion of darkness, its ruler, and all its nefarious purposes.) You can be sure, therefore, that he will make things unpleasant for you.

In doing so, Satan uses the unsaved world of which you once were a part to lure you away from your new commitments, and he will appeal to the "flesh" with which you will have your principal battle within. Framing his words in reminiscence of the first temptation (Genesis 3:6), John warns:

> Everything that is in the world—the desire of the flesh, and the desire of the eyes, and the pride of possessions—is not from the Father but is from the world (1 John 2:16).

And he declares: "Don't be surprised, brothers, if the world hates you" (1 John 3:13). But he also assures us, "... the One Who is in you is greater than the one who is in the world" (1 John 4:4b), so that it is possible to say "... whoever is born of God defeats the world" (1 John 5:4a).

Obviously, these words indicate the existence of a war from which the believer ultimately emerges victorious. But he will not do so without wounds and scars. He must fight in order to "defeat" the evil one.

Indeed, Jesus said, "In the world you will have affliction, but have courage; I have overcome the world"
(John 16:33). You can defeat the world because *He*
has done so, and for no other reason. In one sense
that is the sole message of this book.

The world, as arranged by the evil one, is your
enemy. It appeals to your desires, urging you to
gratify the flesh and covet what you see, and tempts
you to think more highly of yourself than you ought
to think (because of position or possessions). Of
course, the world is only the *means* which the tempter ✓
uses; he himself is the real enemy.

But the Spirit within, and the new heart you received, are set against the sinful gratification of your
desires. They are arrayed in force to combat the
intrusion of the enemy, who Peter warns is "poised
against your soul like an expeditionary force" (1 Peter 2:11b).

Clearly it was conversion itself, in the very nature
of the case, that brought the war into your inner life.
Prior to that time you were like the many today who,
oblivious of their peril, lie peacefully "in the grip of
the evil one" (1 John 5:19).

But why should you be surprised at the preva-
lence of conflict? Look at the life of Jesus, of Peter, of
John, or of Paul. What you see is *conflict*—conflict
seemingly unremitting to the end. Conflict is common to the true church of Christ (1 Peter 5:9b).

Yet do not despair, but rejoice! The presence of
war raging within is evidence of your salvation. And ✓
it provides a wonderful opportunity for you to show
your gratitude to the Savior for what He has done
for you. Put on the armor, take up the sword of the
Spirit, and stride forth into battle for His glory.

4

What's the War Like?

Already something of the nature of the conflict has been described, but it is now time to concentrate our discussion on that matter. Not all wars are alike. Some involve conventional forces, others special-combat groups, etc. Some are fought largely on land and others principally in the air or on the seas. All-out world wars are fought at every level, using every sort of resource.

The war between the seeds is total war. There are no limitations on the extent of the battles, the type of war fought, the weapons the enemy uses, or anything else. How, then, can we know what he is up to in order to defend ourselves and to defeat him in battle?

While it is true that the war is expansive and the enemy is clever, he has preferences and works in patterns that occur again and again. Paul says, "We aren't ignorant of his designs" (2 Corinthians 2:11). In that passage Paul urges certain precautions so that the enemy "won't be able to gain an advantage over us." This reasoning obviously indicates that Paul believed he could anticipate probable enemy maneuvers. If so, it must be possible to discern standard practices that would alert one to possible enemy moves in various situations. Otherwise Jesus' warning to "*watch* [be awake, be on the alert] and pray or you will enter into temptation" (Matthew 26:41) would have little force. If it were not possible for an alert Christian to discern the enemy moving in for the attack, how could you obey the command?

✓ Paul clearly believed that alertness, combined with prayerful study of enemy tactics recorded in the Scriptures, would enable the faithful to avoid the dangers of unnecessary conflicts and successfully prepare for attacks that should not be avoided. Hear him again: "...we aren't ignorant of his designs." This means that Paul thought of his work, in part at least, as warfare. It seems that in all he did, and in all he advised his churches to do, he kept the enemy in mind, anticipating and preparing to counter his most likely moves. There is hope for you, therefore, if you too can learn something of how Satan wages war, so that you may recognize his maneuvers, plan to avoid unnecessary confrontations, and properly resist those in which you must engage. The problem today is that, unlike Paul, many Christians are ignorant of Satan's ploys and consequently step blithely into any number of his many traps. Have you had that sort of problem? What do you know of Satan's designs?

The word translated "designs" (or "devices") in 2 Corinthians 2:11 is literally "the products of one's mind." What Paul is saying, therefore, is that Christians who become well acquainted with God's Word will soon learn how Satan thinks. As a result, they should become aware of the sorts of plans and tactics a mind like his would devise, enabling them to anticipate and guard against his attacks.

The Bible tells us much about Satan and his designs. There you can read directly what God says about the enemy; you can study his crafty plans and purposes used to fight the seed of the woman over the years. You can see God's saints discouraged and defeated, victorious and triumphant, and learn how to avoid failures that led to the defeats while emulating those that brought about the triumphs.

It is important to know that such information is available—that you can become aware of Satan's "designs." Contrary to the unbiblical thinking of many, you are not at his mercy. You can learn when it is appropriate to flee (1 Timothy 6:11; 2 Timothy 2:22), when you are required to resist (James 4:7; 1 Peter 5:9), how to make prudent moves that will keep him from gaining an advantage (2 Corinthians 2:11), and how to avoid giving the enemy a toehold through careless living (Ephesians 4:27).

What Are Satan's Regular Patterns?

In his book *The Divine Unfolding of God's Plan of Redemption* (referred to earlier), James R. Graham lists two major satanic tactics: murder and mixture. Indeed, he thinks that the entire Old Testament history can be read in terms of these two tactics: 1) how Satan either tries to kill off the godly seed through whom God was working His purposes (cf. the evil one's attack upon, and God's providential preservation of, the infant Moses), and in particular the line of Christ, or 2) how he weakens the people with the "mixed multitudes" (who tempt the Jews to murmur and rebel) and by the many compromises with idolatry and alliances with Egypt, Assyria, etc. that tempted them to sin.

It is Graham's astute observation that history has

shown, both in Old Testament times and throughout the church age, with only a few exceptions (for example, Islam's takeover of the once-strong North African church), that mixture has succeeded and murder has failed. Certainly in our own day this seems to be true on the whole.

So there are two patterns in the global battle that may be applied (with some adaptation) to the inner warfare as well. Take mixture, perhaps the more adaptable of the two. Harry Blamires says:

> Nothing has been more damaging to the Christian cause during the last fifteen or twenty years than the assumption by some Christians that there is something outmoded in the notion of conflict between the Church and the World.[1]

In other words, he contends that through education, the media, etc. we have taken the world into the church as if there were no conflict, no antithesis, no difference between her values, goals, and methods and our own. That is mixture. But why is this possible? Because individual Christians have failed to develop a Christian mind. That is to say, they are losing ideological and moral battles within, and thus they easily fall prey to the enemy's propaganda. Take, for example, recent Operation Rescue activities mounted against abortion. While I sympathize with the goals of those who participate, it is clear that they have adopted worldly, carnal tactics introduced into this country by Gandhi that lead them to disobey a good law. Christians, according to Scripture, must disobey the law only when *required* by law to sin. Trespassing laws do not do that. Thus, the outer conflict with evil is carried on by gaining media attention, and by force—all because inner ideological battles have been fought and lost.

Or, take the Christian who abuses his daughter sexually. This happens only after wallowing for long periods in self-pity on the inner battlefield.

Consider the recent emphasis on activism—politically or otherwise—sweeping the church. While citizens must exercise their rights, they can do so to such an extent that the preaching of the gospel is neglected as inconsequential. Satan rejoices over this because he knows that, in the long run, it is only when men and women are brought over to the Lord's side that genuine progress against his efforts takes place. He enjoys granting the church minor outer victories, so long as he can thereby divert her time and attention from the proclamation of the truth. So, by muddling her thinking about this, he wins enormous victories within. It would take too much space here to list the many ways in which Christians have been weakened, but above all else it has been by becoming eclectic (which is simply another way of saying "worldly-minded"). Perhaps this eclecticism can be seen most clearly in counseling (which has been taken captive by psychological theory), in church administration (where worldly business principles and practices have been adopted wholesale), and in missionary and church growth strategies (in which sociological demographic approaches prevail). These areas are as obvious as any, but discerning Christians will see that a mixture of Christian and worldly thinking pervades the church at *all* levels, from the education of our children[2] to the building of our families.

All these compromises, leading to mixtures that weaken the fighting capacity of the church, begin with battles lost in the inner life of individual Christians. Often this mixture begins with the leaders of the church—teachers in colleges and seminaries, pastors in churches, and Christian celebrities who have the money to dominate the daily thinking of many Christians through the media. Of course, if individual Christians were awake to the ways in which the enemy works, and knew the truths of the Scriptures well, they would not allow even trusted leaders to lead them astray; instead, they would search the Scriptures daily to see whether what they hear is so (Acts 17:11). They would know that false teachers attack not only from *without* but from *within* the church itself. And they would soon become adept at reading between the lies (Acts 20:29-31a). But they lack discernment;[3] they have not been "alert," as Paul advised (Acts 20:31). They have been "at ease in Zion," and as a result they readily swallow much that is taught by "angels of light" (2 Corinthians 11:14). Because they are lazy and uninstructed, according to their superficial and unbiblical evaluation "it sounds good."

Murder is not quite so easy to discover in the inner battles of the individual Christian. But it is there nevertheless. As Satan tempts Christians to assent to practices of eating, drinking, smoking, and taking of harmful prescription drugs to counter the effects of sinful lifestyles he is often even more successful than in his outer persecution of the church. Direct persecution tends to weed out those not genuine and to put the true church on her mettle. As Tertullian once said, "The blood of the martyrs becomes the seeds of the church." These abusive practices, along with poor scheduling, worry (which the caring heavenly Father has forbidden), discouragement, depression, bitterness, and a host of other practices that wear us down and make us ineffective (while hastening our deaths), do abound. And as surely as suicide is self-murder, such sins are also all violations of the command not to murder. The Christian has a special concern to preserve his body as much as he can in a world in which it will deteriorate soon enough without his help: It is the temple of the Holy Spirit, which he must not defile. Because Satan wants ineffective Christians who are disobedient to God's law against murder (thereby dishonoring and grieving the Spirit), he does attack the Christian by tempting him to disobey God in such ways.

Other Patterns

While Graham's description of the two major designs of Satan is helpful, it is not completely adequate. It is also important to understand the methods by which the enemy characteristically wages war. Let me mention two: 1) lying and deception, and 2) temptation. I have listed these separately not simply because they must be added to what has been said above, but because in a sense they are not so much strategies of war as they are the principal satanic methods for leading Christians into the compromises of mixture and self-murder. It is by believing his lies that Adam and Eve fell and the entire human race (Jesus excepted) has ever since accepted lies for truth.

It is by failing to "guard" our gardens against intrusions by which he spreads his doubts and denials that we too have allowed the enemy the access he needs to deceive us.

Unlike Adam, who was originally perfect, there is still much in the believer to which the evil one may appeal: evil desires and sin in the members (about which we must speak in detail at a later point). So temptation proves to be his strong weapon. Indeed, these two methods (or tools, if you like) are so much a part of the enemy's usual pattern of waging war that God calls him "the tempter" (Matthew 4:3 KJV; 1 Thessalonians 3:5) and "the deceiver of the whole inhabited world" (Revelation 12:9).

By employing error (usually mixed freely with truth) he "blinds minds" (2 Corinthians 4:4) and comes near to "misleading" even God's chosen ones (Matthew 24:24). Through false prophets he lures many believers to accept strange and destructive teaching (2 Corinthians 11:13-15; 1 John 4:1; Hebrews 13:9; 1 Timothy 4; 2 Peter 2:1) and beguiles others by "lying powers and signs and wonders" (2 Thessalonians 2:9). Every Christian has battles to fight in his inner thought-life against such onslaughts of error and falsehood. There can be no compromise.

Temptation to follow one's mere *desires* (even when these are not evil in and of themselves) rather than his God-given *responsibilities* is always present. It is this temptation to which 1 John 2:16 (among a host of similar warnings) refers: ". . . the desire of the flesh, and the desire of the eyes, and the pride of possessions." Error is often readily accepted because it provides seeming justification for continuing sinful practices, so that both of Satan's methods—

deceit (here self-deceit) and temptation—operate in tandem.

"But how do these designs and methods work out in actual cases?" In the next chapter we will take a close look at some typical instances.

__ 5 _____

Some Cases in Point

Mildred's Inner Struggle

Mildred, a young Christian who is weak in the faith, is a ripe candidate for temptation and deception. She has already been compromised, falling for the devil's lies mediated through unsaved companions (cf. 1 Corinthians 15:33), and in particular Rob, who has gotten her pregnant. She has engaged in deception and lies toward her parents and she has rebelled against all she knows to be right, but now she is in trouble. Yet over the last few rebellious months she has already become adept in self-deceit, telling herself (and getting confirmation from her unsaved friends) that what she desires is what is right. But now the tests have come back positive; the fruit of her sin is apparent. Her friends say, "No problem; get an abortion. Everybody does. You don't even have to tell your parents about it." What should she do?

Lying is one thing, but now her lies, rebellion, and self-deceit have brought her to a point that she never thought she would reach: "I can hardly believe it. Here I am thinking about committing murder! I am actually sitting here wondering whether I should have that precious, little, helpless life snuffed out as if it were a candle! I can't believe myself. What has happened to me?"

What *has* happened to Mildred? She has been compromised and confused through *mixture*. Through her "friends" she has become thoroughly indoctrinated with the world's thinking and the world's ways. And, as God says, the world's ways and thoughts are not the same as His (Isaiah 55:8,9). Is there any hope for her?

Mildred *is* a Christian—a very disobedient one, but nevertheless a Christian in whom the Spirit dwells. That is why she is about to fight the biggest inner battle of her life!

How will the battle go? It depends. Will she continue to listen to Satan's "friendly" advice freely doled out by her friends, all of whom serve in his army? Or will she turn away from them and seek help from her parents, her youth director, or her pastor? And if she does, will she truly repent and take the actions that God requires? Even if she takes the right course of action, what will her motive be? Will it be to preserve the life of a child for fear of living with a conscience that will continually accuse her of murder? Or will she take the hard but proper path of repentance and a change of lifestyle because this incident has brought her to her senses? Will she turn from her sin and her companions—including Rob—because she now wants to please God more than others and herself?

Thoughts like these rush through her mind. Her friends tug one way; the Spirit within tugs another. She is weak; her rebellion has sapped much of her moral strength. She even has a hard time thinking straight. She doesn't want to give up her friends.

"Perhaps Rob will marry me and become a Christian!" she unrealistically tells herself. "And what if I abandon him and keep this child—will I ever find a husband? I might give up the baby for adoption, but could I? Really? That would be so hard. What will people think of me if I carry the baby to term? Could I face the humiliation? I don't think I could ever go back to my church or my youth group again. What will my parents do when they hear? But I can't murder the baby; would God ever forgive me if I did? And I'm no murderess.... What shall I do?"

Mixture! A mixture of values, of motives, of thought. How insidious it is! Satan is good at mixture.

How desperately Mildred needs to cleanse her mind of the devil's error and put on the whole armor of God. She is not prepared to fight this battle. She is alone on the battlefield, with no encouragement from those who could help; she is unacquainted with the wiles of the devil and is a prime target for even greater sin. But even if she were not in such a dreadful spiritual condition, she couldn't fight in her own wisdom and strength. As we shall see later, only the Spirit can enable us to understand His Word and act in accordance with it, by His strength. That is how the Lord's battles are won. Mildred is far from biblical knowledge and even from help in obtaining it, and she lacks the needed strength to overcome the evil one. She has been playing footsy with the enemy for far too long. She is a pushover for evil, a sucker for sin—or is she?

Yes and no. Again, she is far from the Lord, so she has few resources. But if she should genuinely repent, seek God's forgiveness for her rebellion and sin, and seek help from the Lord in prayer and from the Bible (or from the counsel of those in her church or home who could assist her in doing so), she could turn everything around immediately. God says:

> Let the wicked forsake his way, and the unrighteous man his thoughts; and let him return to the Lord, and He will have compassion on him (Isaiah 55:7 NASB).

As a matter of fact, this entire experience—which now looms as a potential tragedy of the most ominous sort—could be turned into a glorious triumph. Indeed, it could be the beginning of a truly vital relationship to Christ. Paul put it this way: "Where sin abounded, grace far more abounded" (Romans 5:20). God is in the business of turning tragedies into triumphs. The cross of Jesus Christ ever stands as a sturdy witness to this fact.

Brad's Battle

Take another all-too-typical scenario. Brad is the Christian husband of a hateful and unbelieving wife. The continual dripping of the shrews mentioned in Proverbs are like the music of a bubbling brook in comparison. Ever since Brad became a Christian and altered much of his lifestyle to accord with his faith, Sally (his wife) has not only continually made fun of him, embarrassing him before all their friends, but has also worked hard at making life as miserable as possible for him. Indeed, to top it all of, over a year ago she even stopped having sexual relations with him. Not only was that bad enough in itself, but during that time she has made a point of titillating him and then refusing to satisfy him.

Brad knows what he must do as a Christian. He must continue to hold up his part of the marriage vows as fully as possible, because he made the promise before God. God has not failed him; it is his wife who has. And since she is not a Christian, it is only to be expected that she would disapprove of his new-found faith. After all, he is no longer the man she married. If he lives as God requires—to please Him—and seeks to obey and honor God in the relationship, he will succeed whether Sally becomes a Christian or not, because he has pleased God. And he knows that this is the prime thing. His peace and happiness do not depend on Sally and her moods but on the faithfulness of God.

"But it's so hard," he tells himself. "If only I had some encouragement from her! If only I could see some inkling of a change in her. But day after day, week after week she is the same, except that she seems to be getting worse. I'm having a terrible time keeping my thoughts and actions pure!"

That's his battle. Inside, though down deep he knows God's answer, he asks, "Would God deny me a little sexual release on the side? Doesn't he want me to be normal, like all the rest of the believers at church? He knows that my capacity for self-control is small. And what harm would it do, anyway?"

There are several women at work with whom Brad is sure he could have an affair. Indeed, one of them, a fairly attractive secretary down the hall in another office, has often made what could only be understood as suggestive remarks. Until now Brad has let them fall flat, simply not taking them up.

Should he grab hold of the next remark and see where it might lead? Or should he even initiate something? Such thoughts, and dozens like them, continually surge through his mind.

Brad is wallowing in self-pity, and that is dangerous. Self-pity is the stuff of which the rationalization of sin is made. Instead of heading in a wholesome direction where he could find strength and help in time of need, he is flirting with disaster. Indeed, as a prelude to peril he has even taken up the practice of looking at pornographic materials on the sly, and lately he has attended several salacious movies. Masturbation has long since become an outlet, and that practice has so escalated his focus on sex that he can hardly think of anything else.

Brad is in trouble. He is at war, and may end up a casualty. It would help him to remember that this is war, that the struggles he is enduring are part of the overall war between the seeds, that God's Name and honor are at stake. You hardly expect easy times on a battlefield. Christ calls His soldiers to "endure hardness" (2 Timothy 2:3 KJV). There is no place for self-pity in a war.

One of Brad's basic problems is that he fails to see his difficulty in military terms. He needs to recognize the secretary down the hall for what she is—a ruse of the enemy to bring him down. Or, as the writer of Proverbs put it, she is a deep pit and a treacherous well into which, if he pursues that course, he will stumble and may drown (Proverbs 23:27). He must come to the realization that pornographic materials and films are enemy propaganda. To give them the time of day—let alone to recall with relish the lurid scenes he has viewed—is near treason. And to indulge in masturbatory self-satisfaction of sexual urges is sin. His body exists for the satisfaction of his marriage partner alone (1 Corinthians 7:4).

Framing his whole experience with the proper biblical parameters of warfare makes a great difference in every way. If he does this, Brad will recognize that the weapons of his warfare cannot be fleshly, and that the mighty weapons of God are at hand (2 Corinthians 10:4). He claims that he has little self-control. Self-control is the fruit of the Spirit (Galatians 5:23). What better circumstances could there be to cultivate and utilize that fruit than those in which he finds himself? Indeed, could it be that this is precisely what the entire battle is all about? If only he will rely upon the Lord, His Word, His weapons, and His people, Brad can win a great victory for Christ. And he personally will grow immensely through it. But if he persists in the course he is now following, there will lie ahead disgrace for him, dishonor to the Name of Christ, and loss of a witness that could in the end win Sally to the Lord.

In these two examples of inner warfare you can readily see murder and mixture at work. Satan literally wants Mildred's baby murdered; he wants to turn her into a murderess. He wants her to injure her body with an abortion, to carry the crushing weight of her sin throughout the days to come, destroying her health. All along the line, by the poor advice of her friends, by her focus on herself rather than on God and her sin against Him, and by appealing to habits of self-deceit and lies which might readily be activated again, Satan is tempting her to go on sinning. Indeed, he is trying to lead her from bad to worse.

What will she do? What would you do? Can you handle temptation? Can you fight the battles of the Lord with an eye trained on *Him* rather than yourself? Can you recognize the designs of the evil one so as to avoid them? Do you know where to find help? Would you avail yourself of it? Like Mildred, do you suffer from the confusion of a mixed-up mind?

These questions are vitally important whether or not you ever face exactly the same experience as Mildred or Brad. You too are in the battle. There is always a war within to win before you can win the battles without. How well are you trained in spiritual warfare? Is it time for you to think through your task on the battlefield and how the battles rage around and within you? Do you even think of day-by-day experiences as encounters with the enemy? Would it make a difference—as we saw in Brad's case—if you did? If nothing else, my hope is that this book will start you thinking along the lines of biblical warfare. The fact that so many of us seldom think about our lives, our problems, and our decisions in military terms accounts for a great deal of the flabbiness of the present-day church.

Rarely has Christ's church in any age had more members, more resources, more wealth, more freedom, and more opportunities to press the battle home to the enemy than now. This is true not only in America but in much of the world. And yet how ineffective she is! How little impact she makes! What is the problem? There are members of the Lord's army strewn all over the battlefield who don't know what hit them. Why? because they don't even know that they are at war. And, not knowing, they take inadequate precautions to protect themselves from danger because they know little or nothing of the enemy's ways or how to combat them. They are inexperienced in warfare and the use of spiritual weapons. They are an army unprepared for war. Perhaps worst of all, when they finally awaken to the fact of global war between the seeds, they fail to understand that this war can be successfully fought only by those who are winning the war within.

It is time to sound the trumpet and summon the troops for action. We had better sound reveille, or we may soon be playing taps.

6

The Enemy's Power

There are always two dangers in this warfare, each as dangerous as the other: You can underestimate the enemy or you can overestimate his power. Both errors have been rife in the church, often at the same time. Usually, however, one or the other predominates.

At times Satan was ignored, his actual existence was doubted, or he was made fun of—usually by depicting him as a ludicrous creature with horns, a tail, and a pitchfork who was dressed in red flannel underwear. Together with such tomfoolery went strange ideas of the devil running hell just as God runs heaven.

Today, in the aftermath of a tidal wave of irrationalism, we find the church inundated with false teachings that grossly overestimate Satan's power. Not only do many Christians cringe in fear of the devil (something he must delight to see), but they dream up all sorts of extrabiblical teachings about the power of the demons who serve him. Some even go so far as to teach that an *unclean* spirit could inhabit a Christian alongside of the *Holy* Spirit. Nothing I know comes so near to the unpardonable sin as such false teaching.*

If there is much confusion about the enemy (and doubtless the devil likes to have it that way), it is important for us to come to a clear understanding of biblical teaching about him. If we must fight with the kingdom of darkness, contend with principalities and powers, and overcome the world, we must know something of the extent of their power and authority.

Satan Is Powerful

From what is said of his activities in the Bible, and from the warnings that the Bible gives about him, we certainly would be foolish to consider the devil of no account. We are told that because he has been cast down to earth, together with his angels, he has "come down to you in a great rage" (Revelation 12:12b). And Peter calls us to be "level-headed and wide awake" because the devil "prowls around like a roaring lion searching for somebody to devour" (1 Peter 5:8). It seems that the ferocity of the enemy is only intensified by the fact that he has been defeated and thrown out of the heavens. Like a wounded

---

* The unpardonable sin was committed by the Pharisees, who attributed the works that the Holy Spirit wrought through Jesus to Beelzebub (another name for Satan). See Matthew 12:24ff. The distinction between "oppression" and "possession" that is made by some must be rejected as exegetically untenable. In the one passage where the word "oppressed" (literally "overpowered") is used (Acts 10:38), it is in a summary statement that refers to Jesus' work of casting out demons as it is recorded throughout the Gospels.

lion, all the more dangerous because he sees that his end is near, Satan strikes out in desperate blows at whomever he can.

So, although the strong man (Satan) has been bound (Matthew 12:29), Christ has triumphed over his minions and disarmed them (Colossians 2:15), and even though Satan is a defeated foe (Hebrews 2:14,15; Revelation 12:7-12), he is still a formidable enemy whose final end has not yet come. In the period that remains, he has determined that if he cannot defeat the armies of heaven, he will make war on the saints (Revelation 12:17).

Jude is explicit in his words about Satan. In spite of his fall and degradation, Jude still ranks him among the "glorious beings" and warns against making "insulting accusations" against him (Jude 8,9). Yet in many so-called "deliverance" meetings today, preachers scream invectives at him, and laugh and poke fun at him in sermons. That is dangerous business, which in time may bring them into greater peril than if, like Michael the archangel, they treated him with respect (Jude 9). We have seen the fall of at least one of the televangelists who made it a practice to do these very things. By indulging themselves in such activities, they place themselves alongside these heretical persons against whom Jude warns— those who "insult whatever they don't understand" (Jude 10).

Satan is powerful, and so long as he remains in his present relationship to us we must respect his authority, even though he misuses it. All authority comes from God. Paul made it clear that Christians were to respect the Roman emperors because of the authority God gave them, even though he must have disapproved of their sinful abuse of it (Romans 13:1-7). And Peter urged recognition of legitimate authority in the home, the state, and elsewhere (1 Peter 3:1-7,13-17), even when it was being misused. Similarly, we must recognize the remnants of authority, such as they may be, that the devil yet retains.

Luther put it well when he wrote in his hymn, "his power and craft are great." The devil is by nature more powerful than human beings, and he is too crafty for us to withstand unaided in our debilitated, sinful state. That is also why we must be wary of him. Spurgeon wrote:

> He is more cunning than the wisest: How soon he entangled Solomon! He is stronger than the strongest: How fatally he overthrew Samson! Yes, and men after God's own heart, like David, have been led into most grievous sins by his seductions.[1]

But His Power Is Limited

Yet having said that, we must remember that the devil is not all-powerful. If it is wrong to show disrespect for his authority and power, or disregard them as threats, it is also wrong to cringe in fear before him. We are told, "The One Who is in you is greater than the one who is in the world" (1 John 4:4). The Holy Spirit in you is far more powerful than the devil. Whenever Jesus approached demons, it was they who cringed. There is a great difference between recognizing genuine danger and cowering before it in servile fear.

Although the devil has come down to the earth in a great rage, he is not invincible: The overcoming saints "defeated him by the Lamb's blood and by the word of their testimony" through remaining steadfast "even to [a martyr's] death" (Revelation 12:11). The world, Satan's domain, is powerful, but Jesus said:

> In the world you have affliction, but have courage; I have conquered the world (John 16:33).

While the task is formidable, John declares:

> ...whoever has been born of God defeats the world. And this is what defeats the world: our faith. Who can defeat the world except those who believe that Jesus is God's Son? (1 John 5:4,5).

God does not want you to cower or grovel before the evil one. He expects you to be victorious over Satan, his world, and the host of demons who from time to time may tempt you to sin. If you resist the evil one, as you are commanded, while "standing firm in the faith" (1 Peter 5:9), he will flee from you (James 4:7).

It is important to gain the proper biblical perspective on this matter because many people today excuse their sinful behavior by claiming "the devil made me do it." That is never true of a Christian. He is not one of the devil's toadies. There is never an excuse for sinning. He could have resisted temptation. Have you fallen prey to some such excuse? It too is a lie of the evil one that you must immediately reject if you would win the war within. He would like you to believe that you are helpless, that he can so overcome you that you are mere putty in his hands. He wants you to curl up and submit to his temptations, offering no resistance. By accepting such unbiblical teaching, no wonder so many Christians are losing the war!

I recently read the preliminary copy of an otherwise very helpful book that was flawed only by the statement that Satan put certain ideas into the author's mind. She claimed that she could never have thought such sinful things otherwise. I do not care to disclose the name of the author or book, because I have written her about the matter, and have hopes she will see fit to change her statement.

But here it is—the view that Satan may have direct influence over our thoughts (and according to others) our actions. Is that true?

Well, from my comments about the book mentioned above, you know I think not. But why? There are several reasons. First, all that has been said thus far contradicts the notion. Second, Jesus in the Sermon on the Mount, as well as elsewhere, explicitly made a point of the fact that we would be held accountable for our thought life. If it can be controlled by another being, that is not possible. But third—and this is the clincher—John tells us:

> ...whoever has been born of God doesn't sin [i.e., as the unsaved person does], but the One born of God [Jesus Christ] keeps him, and the evil one doesn't touch him (1 John 5:18).

Here God plainly tells you that if you have been

born again Jesus "keeps" ("guards and protects")
you from the evil one. Is Satan stronger than Christ,
who stands between you and the evil one? "No," you
say, "but I can remove myself from that protection,
can't I?" No, you cannot. But, even granting the
possibility, look at the rest of the verse: The evil one
can't even "touch" the believer.

These are precious words. This promise ought to
be echoed and reechoed among Christians. It means
that the devil's power is limited to spreading lies and
tempting you through outward means alone. He
cannot take possession of you or of your mind. He
cannot directly introduce thoughts into your head.
He cannot *make* you do anything. On the one hand,
while this truth removes all excuse-making, on the
other hand it gives great hope and comfort to those
who warmly embrace it. Think of it: There is nothing that the devil can do but try to influence you
through the world and by appealing to your own
desires!

The word "touch" (*hapto*) used by John is the same
word found in the Septuagint (Greek) translation
of Job 1:11,12; 2:5, where it is recorded that Satan
found it necessary to ask permission to "touch" (lay
hold of or grasp) Job's possessions and ultimately his
body. Even there his power is seen to be limited. But
though Satan was granted permission in Job's case
(a very special one), John, doubtless alluding to that
incident, say this will never happen to you. He cannot lay a hand on you. How good to know that fact!

Moreover, Satan is a finite creature. He has neither omniscience (complete knowledge) nor omni-
presence (the ability to be everywhere at once); nor
is he all-powerful (omnipotent), as we have just seen.

Like us, he is subject to his Creator. He is in no way equal to God. This means that all the temptation that is going on in the world is not the work of Satan himself. Much of it comes from his earthly followers, who are called in John's writings "the world." Some of the temptation may at times stem from the work of some demon or other. Rarely would you encounter Satan himself. Probably he is most active where the battle rages hottest against him.

✓ You must remember that there is nothing the devil could tempt you to do that you couldn't tempt yourself to do. Our lady author, mentioned previously, has far too sanguine a view of the human mind. As a matter of fact, when James comments on temptation (in the most definitive biblical passage on the subject) he does not even mention the devil in conjunction with it. Rather, he writes: "...each one is tempted *by his own desires*" (James 1:14a).

It is to *the enemy within* that Satan, the world, and the demons must make their appeal—through the eyes, the flesh, and the pride of life (1 John 2:16). If you would draw closer to the war within, you must come to grips with this enemy within: It is he whom you must dread. This enemy agent living within God's territory is perhaps responsible for as much damage to the Lord's troops as Satan and all his hosts. He is a saboteur par excellence; he was Paul's principal enemy, and is probably yours as well. You need to become acquainted with him and his ways. You must learn how to overcome him if you would win the war within.

Because of the important place he plays in the war within, we must devote the entire next chapter to a description of the enemy within and of the ways in which he carries on his nefarious campaign.

__ 7

The Enemy Within

Speaking of the Christian warrior, Phillips Brooks once said, "...he must struggle to know who his true enemy is, and to fight finally with him alone."[1] That enemy, known by any number of code names, is what they call in espionage terminology a "mole"— someone who has penetrated deeply into the very vitals of every Christian. And that enemy is *the flesh*. *You* are your own worst enemy!

Referring to the battles without and within, John Calvin said of the latter:

> This is the principal war in which God would have his people to be engaged. He would have them strive to suppress every rebellious thought and feeling which would turn them aside from the path to which he points. And the consolations are so ample that it may well be said we are more than cowards if we give way.[2]

These two preachers understood that you must grapple with the real enemy. Satan and demons and the world are genuine, formidable foes. I would not discount them in any way. But it is impossible to defeat them until the interior battle with the self is fought and won.

Brooks continues, speaking of every great Christian soldier on the broader battlefields of life who from time to time has

> ... shut the door upon all the tumult of the world and left the great cause for an hour to take care of itself, while he fought with himself for himself—with himself his own enemy.... There are verses enough, you know, in St. Paul's Epistles which let us see that struggle with himself going on all the time underneath the other struggle with the men of Jerusalem and Athens. While the foreign war was raging, the home country also was all up in arms.[3]

The battle within, in the end, is nothing less than a battle for self-conquest.

Is it really responsible counsel then to say to one who comes beaten and battered by sin, "Go"—go back to the battlefield—"Go, and sin no more" (John 5:14). Can he? Is it possible to overcome the sin that for so long has been his master?

Romans Six

Brooks mentioned it and we must understand it—in some detail. It is the war within that Paul described in Romans 6 through 8, but especially in chapters 7 and 8. About what is Paul speaking when he tells us in Romans 7:14-25 of the misery and defeat he suffered? Are we all doomed to cry out with him, "What a miserable person I am! Who will rescue me from this body of death?" (verse 24)? Is that the epitome of Christian living and Christian warfare?

No, because in the very last verse he answers his own question: "Thank God, it is Jesus Christ our Lord Who will [rescue me]" (verse 25). Whatever this struggle may be, it is not the struggle of one who can gain no victories. He is surely describing a situation in which he failed to call upon the available resources to be found in Christ Jesus. Let us examine the passage closely to try to see what Paul is talking about. To do so, we shall have to go back and approach it in context.

In chapters 6 to 8 several matters are in view. One is the believer's identification with Christ. In Romans 5:20 Paul had discussed justification by faith, and declared God's grace to be far greater than all our sin. In chapter 6 he begins by taking up a possible objection to that declaration: "If grace is poured out more freely than sin, then why not sin more so that we can receive even more grace than now?"

"No," Paul answers, "let it not be so!" The thing is unthinkable. You are in Christ, he says. Therefore, you must recognize that you are "dead to sin but living for God" (verse 11). How is this? His explanation is found in verses 1-5. The Christian is so identified with Christ that all He did is accounted to him. When he was baptized with the Holy Spirit, he was baptized into Christ. That is to say, he became so identified with Him that all Christ did was accounted to him. He was counted to be circumcised with Christ (Colossians 2), crucified with Christ, buried with Christ, risen with Christ, and seated in the heavenly places with Christ (Colossians 3:1).

To be "in Christ" is like putting a bean in a pot. Wherever the pot goes the bean goes too, because it is in the pot. Put the pot on the floor and the bean is on the floor, because it is in the pot. Put the pot on the table and the bean is on the table, because it is in the pot. Whatever Christ did we are counted to have done because we are *in Him.*

Because we are "baptized into Christ" His whole holy record is accounted to us. But Paul selects two parts from the whole that illustrate his main point: We are *buried* and *raised* with Christ. If you have the whole (being baptized into Christ), you also have the parts (death and resurrection) that illustrate the fact that you have died to your former way of life and now live to serve God instead of sin. Legally you are no longer the same person; you have a new record, a new identity, and a new relationship.

He now discusses this new relationship. As elsewhere (Colossians 3; Ephesians 4), Paul moves from what Christians *are* in Christ to what they *ought to be* (and can be) in daily living (Romans 6:6): from identification to union with Him, from the legal to the experiential. His point is that rather than sin *more*, the opposite ought to be true.

In this discussion he immediately mentions the body—a great concern throughout the rest of this chapter and the next. He sees his body as the cause of all his problems with spiritual growth. Because of the guilt and corruption inherited from Adam, every person born by ordinary generation wrongly habituates his body from his earliest days. There is nothing of Greek gnostic thinking in Paul, thinking that declares the body as such to be the source of sin. With his Savior, Paul would have affirmed that sin seeps into the body from the heart (Matthew 15:11). But he does speak disparagingly of the body (both here and in the next chapter) *as it has been captured and controlled by sin.*

Paul sees a day when the body will be completely freed from all effects of sin, when we shall be raised with a body that is like Christ's glorious body (Philippians 3:21). But in contrast to that future glorious body, it is now a "degraded" body. And here in Romans 6 and 7 it is not only the effects of sin (leading to bodily defects, wear and tear, etc.) that he has in mind. More to the point is the fact that the body has been programmed by one's sinful nature to *sin*. At conversion that programming does not automatically disappear, so that there is an absolutely fresh start. Quite to the contrary—it carries over into the new life, making the body with its desires an enemy within. James puts it this way:

> Where do wars...come from? Isn't it from your pleasures that are warring in your bodily members? (James 4:1).

Calvin writes, "When we shall be stripped of this body, then we shall be stripped of the servitude of sin."[4] Sin is plainly personified as a slave master in verses 12 and 14 of Romans 6, but the *thought* of sin as such is already in Paul's mind in the verses preceding. In exhorting to holiness, Paul recognizes how the body, habituated as it is to sin, gets in the way.

But there is hope. He says that by His death Christ made the body "ineffective" (verse 6). That is to say, sin's hold over the body is no longer absolute. The body, as well as the rest of the person, has been set free from sin's dominion. But the body is still viewed as a "body of sin." In other words, it is a body that, apart from changes made by sanctification (in which new habits replace old ones), still persists in indulging its desires.

Ultimately, therefore, the body cannot hinder us from serving Christ. It will be a constant irritation until death or the coming of the Lord, but it ought to become less and less so as we grow by grace. In verse 6, then, Paul is giving hope. It has now become possible to serve Christ as a new Master rather than to serve sin (verse 6b), bodily desires need no longer dominate us (verse 12), we don't have to be led by the body, and bodily members can be rehabituated to the service of God as instruments (or weapons) of righteousness (verses 13,16,19). Paul, therefore, ends chapter 6 with a great word of emancipation from sin (verses 20-23).

This problem of the body, along with the problem of living in newness of life, occupies Paul's attention for the next two chapters.

Romans Seven

Skipping over the illustration in verses 1-4, where Paul shows us that death freed us from the law's grip, we begin with verse 4. However, it is important to note that the subject of the law (the third concern in these chapters) is reintroduced. In earlier chapters Paul had shown how no one could be saved by the law. Justification had to be by faith. Here he introduces the problem of law in relationship to *sanctification* (becoming more like Christ). In seeing this point correctly lies the answer to many of the difficult questions surrounding verses 14 and following. But first let us look briefly at the intervening section, verses 4-13.

In this discussion Paul shows how the law only

aggravated and exposed his sinful condition when he was without Christ. But it could do nothing to remove that sin from him. Sin got hold of the body, trained it, and used it to serve its own ends (verse 5). The law *exposed* but couldn't *remedy* the situation; only Christ could do that (verses 5,6).

Paul goes on to say that the problem really isn't with the law, which is good (verse 12); it is with *me*. The law was never intended to free me from sin, and so long as I rely on it to do something it was never intended to do, I shall fail. This is the same point he made in Galatians 3:2,3.

We come now to verses 14-25, the critical passage of Romans chapter 7. Well, then, says Paul, if the law is good and I am evil, so that it took the death of Christ to release me from sin's hold, what about now? (Note the shift at verse 14 from the past tense to the present; Paul is writing about the believer *after* conversion, not before.) *Maybe the law couldn't justify, but can it sanctify?* That is the next problem Paul takes up in verses 14-25 (it was suggested as far back as 6:22b).

In verse 14 he sets the theme: I find that though the law is good and spiritual, I am still fleshly, and the law can do nothing to change that fact. When I on my own try to bring about change in order to conform to God's law, I can't do it. *I* am the problem, and the "I" that is the focal point of difficulty is the "I" that centers in my body (there is that concern again about the body that hinders sanctification). My body continues to yearn for "the leeks and garlic of Egypt"! I am led and pulled by the habituated desires of the flesh (what it is accustomed to expect), even though sin is no longer my master. Yet because of my body problem, it is as though I were still under sin's dominion ("sold under sin").

The body is still too much in control of me; *I* should be in control of *it*. It is like the title of C.S. Lewis's book *The Horse and His Boy*, where everything is turned around backward. I find that what I want to do is what I don't do, and what I don't want to do is what I do anyway.

There are two "I's" here:

1. Whenever the "I" is said to do the sinful thing, it is identified with the fleshly body ("nothing good dwells in me"—verse 18; "sin's law that is in my members" [of the body]—verse 23c; flesh identified with sin in members—verse 25).

2. Whenever the "I" evaluates this sinning, it distances itself from the other "I" (verse 17).

Paul is saying that there is something within me that won't identify with the sin in me. This he calls "my mind" (verses 23,25) and the "I" in "my inner person" (verse 22).

He says that the potential for the mastery of my life, including my body, is there (as he said in chapter 6), now that I am in Christ, but too often I lose the battle inside me between my members and the better "I." Why is this? What is the way out?

This happens when Paul (or you, or I) tries to modify his bodily inclinations *in his own strength alone*. This is what Paul speaks of as trying to become "sanctified by the law." The law can no more sanctify than it can save. Here he is showing how the law is totally ineffective in overcoming the tendencies of a sin-habituated body. He states this unequivocally in Romans 8:3, where he makes it clear that because of the flesh it is impossible for the law to accomplish sanctification.

Paul explains that he fails whenever he alone fights battles with his body; look at the combatants in verse 25: "I" and "my flesh." But *Christ in him* can help him win battles. He needs the work of the Holy Spirit within to tilt the scale in favor of his better self. By His indwelling Spirit, Christ will free him from bondage. The Spirit is an Ally greater than the flesh (the body wrongly habituated). Christ dealt with "sinful flesh" by dying in a body that is in the likeness of it, but not wrongly habituated as it is (8:3). He rightly habituated His own body to serve God from the beginning, because He had a sinless nature that always did the will of the Father.

In his book *No More Mr. Nice Guy!* Steve Brown writes:

> Most Christians are trying to be good by their own efforts because a Christian is supposed to be good. A Christian *is* supposed to be righteous. The problem comes when the goodness is a result of nothing but will power. We never have enough will power. Paul said, "For I know that in me (that is, in my flesh) nothing good dwells; for to will is present with me, but how to perform what is good I do not find. For the good that I will to do, I do not do; but the evil I will not to do, that I practice" (Romans 7:18,19). And then Paul cried out (just as every Christian cries out when he or she has only willed to be good), "O wretched man that I am! Who will deliver me from this body of death?" (Romans 7:24).[5]

That about sums it up!

Romans chapter 8 tells the story of battles fought and won as the Spirit leads us in paths of righteousness. The Christian must get out of chapter 7 and into chapter 8, though not as a one-time thing, as if this could be done by some special act which once-for-all meant that all battles henceforth would be properly fought and won. (Some speak of making the transition between the chapters in that way.)

No, this is not a one-time decisive act or crisis event. The reason we know this is that we so often find ourselves straying back into Romans 7. It is part of the very sinful patterns we are fighting to try to battle the enemy without in our own wisdom and strength. We can't, as we have so clearly seen in the last chapter. So every time you find yourself bemoaning the fact that you are doing sinful things you wanted to avoid or failing to keep those good resolutions you made, wake up to the fact that you have wandered back into Romans 7. You are attempting to fight the enemy with your own resources. Whenever you find that your flesh is in control, repent, seek help, and gain the mastery over it.

To summarize: there is one basic contrast (8:4b):

Romans 7	**Romans 8**
Walking according to the flesh (that is, led by the flesh): the wrongly programmed body in control.	Walking according to the Spirit (that is, led by the Spirit); the Spirit in control.

The essential thing to see is that when the battle is rightly fought, the struggle in Galatians 5:16-18:

Now I tell you, walk by the Spirit and it
is certain that you won't accomplish the
desires of the flesh. The flesh's desires are
contrary to those of the Spirit, and the
Spirit's are contrary to those of the flesh.
They are in opposition to one another so
that you don't do what you want to do. But
if you are led by the Spirit, you aren't under
law.

parallels the one depicted in Romans 8 and not the
one in Romans 7. In the final analysis the question is
simply this: When you go over the top to take on the
enemy within, who leads—you or the Spirit? If you
are led by the Spirit, you will prevail; if you are not,
you will experience all the miseries of failure delin-
eated in Romans 7.[6]

__ 8 _____

Fighting with the Spirit's Sword

Success or failure in the war within depends (as we saw in the last chapter) on whether or not a Christian avails himself of the help of the Holy Spirit. God did not give you the Holy Spirit in vain. That was the message of Romans 7 and 8. Paul demonstrated that the law could neither save nor sanctify. Its purpose is to do neither; it satisfies its functions when it becomes a pedagogue or guardian to lead us to Christ (Galatians 3:24), by showing us our need of a Savior and Sanctifier, and by revealing God's standard for righteous living.

But to say that victory in the various battles we fight depends on availing yourself of the Holy Spirit's power is, if nothing more is said, purely nebulous, or at best mystical. That is too often how the matter is left. People wonder, "What does that mean?" "How does one rely upon the Holy Spirit and tap His power?" In this book I intend to answer those questions directly in a concrete and practical way.

To gain some focus on the answer, let's return to Mildred. We left Mildred in a quandary. Her conscience has been seriously dulled by her rebellion and by swallowing the desensitizing lies and deceits of unsaved companions. By her own sinful nature, apart from assistance from anyone, she has also manufactured innumerable rationalizations for her sinful behavior. Yet her conscience is still functioning well enough for her to recognize murder when she sees it. And that is precisely what is staring her in the face—murder in all its bloody ugliness as a live option!

She has become so weakened by her previous life of arrogant debauchery that she hardly has any motivation to resist. Yet as she contemplates the options before her, she remembers her Christian upbringing and the teachings of the Word of God that she learned at home and church. So out of a mixture of fear, sentiment, half-obedience to God, or whatever her true motive may be, she determines not to go through with the abortion. She doesn't know what to do instead, but she says, "I can't do *that*!" Confused, feeling dirty, hoping against hope for another solution, feeling like "a battleground still in dispute,"[1] she tells Rob of her intentions.

Rob: "What? You mean you aren't going to get the abortion? That'll spoil all our fun. You can't really mean it—"

Mildred: "Oh, Rob, it's so awful thinking of taking that little baby's life. I just can't. It would be murder."

Rob: "Now, Mildred, I've told you a hundred times—that's no baby; it's just a piece of tissue. There's no more to an abortion than removing an appendix."

Mildred: "No, Rob, it's a *baby*. I know that much, and I'm *not* going to kill it!"

Rob: "Do you think I'm going to let you go around everywhere telling people I got you pregnant? You're crazy! And what about the baby—what are you going to do with it? It'll spoil everything."

Mildred: "I thought...I thought you might want to marry me, Rob. Then we could raise our child. You'd be a father."

Rob: "A father? Ha! That's a laugh. Me? *Marry* you? Now I know you're crazy. Hey! Wait a minute—is *that* why you want to keep the baby? You want to blackmail me into marriage, don't you? Well, of all the—"

Mildred: "No, Rob, I'm not trying to blackmail you. I simply can't kill our baby."

Rob: "*Our* baby? That's what you think! I'll tell you what you can do: You can take that baby of *yours* home to 'Mommy and Daddy' and that church of yours that you're always talking about, but don't expect *me* to have anything to do with it. Let them figure out what to do with your baby. I'm history!"

Mildred: "Oh, Rob! You said you loved me. I thought—"

Rob: "How dumb can you get, anyway? I'm gone!"

And he was. It took her awhile, but soon Mildred came to her senses in the "far country" and reflected as follows:

Rob and my so-called friends don't really care about me. They've left me cold. I didn't know when I had it so good. I was better off at home, even with all the little hassles. My parents will be hurt, but I've already hurt them so much.... Well, Rob was right about one thing: They do love me and they will know what to do to help me. I'm going home. Anything is better than this—running around with a gang of potential murderers; it will be better even if Mom and Dad make me crawl!

So Mildred goes home. Her parents, who are Christians, are heartbroken because of the sin, but at the same time are thankful that their prayers have been answered by her return. Yet after reconciliation and much crying by everyone all around (no one expected Mildred to "crawl"; cf. Luke 15), when they sat down to face the problem of the baby, no one was sure how to handle it. So they called the pastor.

He made an appointment to see them, and after three counseling sessions with Mildred and her parents, here is what had happened:

1. Mildred was brought to genuine repentance before God.

2. She sought forgiveness from God, her parents, and the elders (representing the congregation), who, hearing her confession, forgave her in the name of the congregation.

3. The elders, on behalf of Mildred, announced to the congregation that Mildred had become pregnant, had confessed her sin against God and man, and had been forgiven. They further instructed the congregation that God expected them to comfort her and reaffirm their love toward her (2 Corinthians 2:7,8), giving her whatever help they could to reassimilate her into the body.

4. They also instructed the congregation that because the matter has been closed through forgiveness, there must be no gossip or avoidance of Mildred, and warned that anyone found doing so might be subject to discipline.

As a result, at the end of the service people came from all over the church building, tears streaming from their eyes to hug Mildred and assure her of their love and concern, welcoming her back into the fellowship of the church. Since then many of these people have made various overtures to help, climaxing their love and concern in a huge baby shower for Mildred and her little one.

What has happened here? Well, look at it this way: The devil was defeated on the battlefield of Mildred's life. Several battles were won. We want to investigate a couple of these to determine how. Remember our earlier concern: How is it that the Spirit enables us to overcome the flesh?

Battles Won

First, there was the battle which Mildred fought about returning home. Humiliated, half-afraid, and still clinging to remnants of her rebellion, Mildred nevertheless won that battle and returned. How come?

Well, in part because of the providential work of God. Rob gave her no real alternative when he revealed his complete lack of concern for her or the baby. And enough of her past Christian training asserted itself to keep her from murdering her baby. She knew that all the assurance of her pagan "friends" that "everyone does it," "that's not a baby— it's just a piece of tissue," and the like were lies. The

Spirit of God within Mildred enabled her to recall and apply the biblical teaching she had received from the pulpit, at home, in Sunday school, and in her youth group. The Spirit helped Mildred to win that battle through His implanted Word.

Next, Mildred knew her parents were Christians and that they loved her and would help her find the right course to take. She knew that somehow, through their prayers and their understanding of the Bible, something would work out. She knew she would hurt them, but they had already been deeply hurt by her rebellion and their Christian faith had nevertheless sustained them. So she went home.

Then, when they went to the pastor, he was able to help in several ways. Through the use of Scripture that he applied to her case, Mildred was brought to repentance. He explained that it wasn't enough to merely escape from the consequences of her sin. He pointed out from the Bible that her sin was first and foremost against God, and that she must recognize this and seek His forgiveness, as well as forgiveness from all the people she had injured. And he explained from the Bible why God requires forgiveness, what forgiveness is, and what it does. Being forgiven made all the difference. Mildred was now in a condition to receive help and guidance for the future. She was also now willing to obey God's commands (a good soldier must be willing to obey orders). That was a great victory.

As the pastor continued to minister the Word, opening it up, explaining it in detail, and applying it concretely to Mildred's situation, the Spirit illumined her mind and enabled her to learn and agree to do whatever was necessary.

Mildred's first inclination was to run away from the consequences of her sin: "Can't I go quietly away for eight months or so, give up the child for adoption, and then return to start my life all over again?" she asked. At first her parents were inclined to agree, because this course would save embarrassment before all their friends. But the pastor wisely said:

> No, you must consider the congregation. You must be forgiven by the congregation because your sin has public dimensions. Not only so, but you need the body during this time—its advice, its encouragement, its instruction, its support. If there is any place where reconciliation can occur it is among the members of the body of Christ. You need us and we need you.

So Mildred was persuaded from the Scriptures to remain among the members of the congregation. In the end she was very glad she did. Many of the women of the church, motivated by Titus 2:3-5, spent time with her, talking helpfully about her situation. In the end, through their guidance, she decided to keep the beautiful blond-haired, blue-eyed boy that God gave her that looked so much like her. Two years later God also sent her a husband. More battles won!

What Dynamic Was at Work?

Having followed this scenario to its completion, think about it a bit more carefully. What happened to Mildred? *When she came under the influence of the*

Word of God she began winning battles. When she returned to the Christian community, she found the Spirit at work everywhere—in the lives of her parents, her pastor, and the members of her church. When she had removed herself from the family of faith, she left most of that influence behind. Not totally, however, because in her extremity the Spirit activated the Word hidden in her heart many years before. Apart from that Word implanted deep within, she would have lost the first battle and hence all that followed it.

At each step, with each new battle, as she fought her way back to God, as she struggled against sinful pride and arrogance, as she reversed foolish actions and decisions, it was *the Bible*—either directly studied or lovingly lived out in the lives of God's people—that protected her from her worst self with all its faulty thinking and sinful tendencies, and helped her to win her way into peace and obedience. What you must see, above all else, in this short vignette, is *the Holy Spirit at work using His Word.*

The Spirit's Sword Slays the Flesh

In Galatians 5:16,18 we read:

> Now I tell you, walk by the Spirit and it is certain that you won't accomplish the desires of the flesh.... But if you are led by the Spirit, you aren't under law.

In this passage we have a brief summary of Romans 8:1-14. The real battle is between *you and the Spirit* on the one side and *the flesh* (the body wrongly habituated toward sin) on the other.* An unregenerate person will always be led around by his flesh, fulfilling the desires of his flesh and his mind (i.e., his sinful thinking). But a spiritual person (i.e., one in whom the Spirit dwells) can be led by the Spirit. Of course, there are times when he isn't, as we see in Mildred's case, and in the passage at which we looked in Romans 7:14,15. But there are also times when he is led by the Spirit through the Word. Anyone who is *ever* led by the Spirit is regenerate, as Romans 8 makes abundantly clear (along with 1 Corinthians 2, to which I referred in an earlier chapter). To be led by the Spirit is to fulfill the law, and thus be pleasing to God and not be under its condemnation. But Paul says that those "who are in the flesh [the unregenerate] cannot please God" (Romans 8:8).

Clearly Mildred had been following a sinful path as she allowed herself to be "led" by the flesh and the world. But when she came under the influence of scriptural teaching and living, she changed direction and began following the Spirit, and He led her in paths of righteousness. Perhaps Jowett crystallized it as well as any other when he said:

> When a man listens to the voice of the tempter within him, he is inclined to do as

---

* Incidentally, notice that neither in Romans 7 and 8 nor in Galatians 5 is the devil or any of his angels mentioned. The fundamental battle is between the Spirit and the flesh. The devil and the world can tempt the flesh, but can do no more. Of course that is quite enough for us, since we have fighting enough to do against the insidious flesh itself.

others do, not to resist when the temptation seems great. But when he looks into the law of God and hears the words of Christ, his natural sense of right and wrong is restored to him, and he becomes elevated, purified, sanctified.[2]

It is important to understand this leading of the Spirit. It has nothing to do with impressions or feelings or direct revelations from God. It is not promptings or checks in the Spirit. No. Every right decision and action that Mildred made was directed by the Spirit *through His Word.* All her poor, sinful decisions and moves were made by listening to the siren voice of her flesh and the deceitful lies of the world that appealed to the flesh. Crucial battles were won or lost by following the Spirit or the flesh. The victories she experienced, as she battled for integrity, were won only when she abandoned all other influences and gave herself up to scriptural ones. Of course, Mildred was largely dependent on other people because at this point she was "inexperienced with the righteous Word" and her "faculties" had not been "trained by practice to distinguish good from evil" (Hebrews 5:13,14).

It is not always clear in modern preaching or writing just *how* the Spirit works. While I have emphasized the point throughout this chapter, let me say it again. I want to leave no one in doubt about the answer: *He works through His Word.* While it is true that he *can* work in other ways (and in times past has done so), He has chosen in this day to work by the Scriptures, of which He (using the personalities and pens of chosen men to write inerrantly) ultimately is the Author. That is why, when exhorting us to fight the battles within, He tells us to take up "the Spirit's sword, which is God's Word" (Ephesians 6:17). Listen to Spurgeon:

> Fight with your sins! Hack them in pieces, as Samuel did Agag. Let not one of them escape. Take them as Elijah took the prophets of Baal—hew them in pieces before the Lord.[3]

Even Jesus, when fighting His battles, did so by the Word that comes forth from His mouth like a Roman broadsword (cf. Revelation 19:15a). It was with Scripture that He met the three temptations of Satan in the wilderness (Matthew 4:1-11).

For thousands of years the Spirit patiently prepared His Word. Now that it is complete, He does not choose to ignore it, but rather uses it for the express purpose of fighting the flesh. He does so by illuminating the believer's mind to understand it (see 1 Corinthians 2 again). He also strengthens us, encouraging us by the Word to follow the Word.

How did I reach such a conclusion? Here are a few grounds for doing so:

1. If the Spirit intends to work apart from His Word, it seems strange that He would have produced it. Remember, the Bible is peculiarly *His* book: Consider 2 Peter 1:18-21. Here He calls us to "pay attention" to "the prophetic Word," as to "a lamp shining in a dismal place" (verse 19) until Christ comes. That is to say, it is the only place where the reader can find enlightenment. All else—dreams, hunches, impressions, feelings—is darkness. He

also says the written Word gives us greater assurance than any legitimate revelatory experience could (verse 19a).

2. In Scripture, the same things are said of the Spirit and the Word, so that the two are identified rather than distinguished. Take a couple of examples. In Hebrews we read, "the Holy Spirit testifies" when the writer quotes the Bible (Hebrews 10:15; see also 4:7). Consider also Romans 15:13:

> Now may the God of hope fill you with every sort of joy and peace in believing, so that you may have an abundance of hope by the power of the Holy Spirit.

and Romans 15:4:

> Whatever was written before was written for our instruction, that by the endurance and the encouragement that the Scriptures give us we may have hope.

How do you get hope? From what source, through what means? If you compare the two verses above you will find that "abundant hope" comes from the "God of hope" (the Source) by the "power of the Spirit" (the Agent). But it is also clear that it is by "the endurance and the encouragement that the Scriptures [the means the Agent uses] give us [that] we may have hope." The two are so closely identified they can be separated only at the reader's peril.

Look at one more passage. In 2 Timothy 3:16 Paul says that the Scriptures "convict." But in John 16:8 Jesus indicates just as surely that conviction is the work of the Spirit. Once more not *contradiction* but *identification* of the two is apparent.

Therefore, when we read of being "led" by the Spirit to walk according to the will of the Lord (Romans 8; Galatians 5), we must recognize that such leading takes place not *apart from* but *through* the Scriptures. The Spirit leads when He enables us to understand and to follow His written Word.

But this doesn't happen automatically. The Spirit is a Person. Your relationship to Him is crucial (He can be "grieved" and "quenched"); it affects His work. If He is offended He cannot be expected to illumine, direct, or strengthen through the Word until there is heartfelt repentance, leading to confession of sin and forgiveness. And He must surely be offended when you fail to turn to His Word for help. Relate properly to God's Spirit; that's how to begin. Then, having won that battle (as in Mildred's case), it is possible to fight others as well.

What must we say then? It is plain that the Word of God, God's truth (John 17:17), sanctifies as the Spirit uses it. Here is the great offensive weapon that every believer must learn to use well. Truth is a weapon stronger than any in the enemy's arsenal. The "father of lies" knows nothing of truth. He lacks the power of truth and cannot withstand it. He has no shield of faith to quench the fiery darts of God's Word! In fighting the Lord's battles you must never use the enemy's weapons. Not only are they ineffective and less powerful than God's, but you will always fail when you do so; the Spirit will not strengthen and use you when you pick up the sword of lying, deceit, or error. If you would resist the evil one so that he will flee from you, flash the Sword of the Spirit (i.e., the weapon He provides and uses), the Sword of truth, in his face.

__ 9 _____

The Believer's Other Weapons

Jesus promised His disciples that the Spirit of truth would lead them into *all* truth (John 16:13). Undoubtedly that promise was fulfilled in the writing of the New Testament Scriptures that completed God's revelation of truth to man. As in Jesus all finally came to its zenith point, so too did the *revelation* concerning Him. The Spirit of truth, as we have seen, helps us to win the war within as we wield the Sword of truth.

When I say that there are other weapons, do not misunderstand: There are no other *revelatory* weapons. In the Bible can be found all things necessary for life and godliness. Nothing more is required or needed. In it you will find truth, guidance, warning, encouragement, counsel, comfort, rebuke, admonishment—all any soldier of Christ would ever need to fight the Lord's battles. Through the Bible, God has equipped us "with every good thing for doing His will" (Hebrews 13:21). But other weapons for fighting the war must accompany the Scriptures if they are to be used with power and effectiveness. In particular, these are faith and prayer.

Prayer

In delineating separate pieces of the believer's

armor Paul mentions prayer, not so much as a weapon but as that element which must accompany all else:

> Do all of this with prayer and petition, praying at all times by the Spirit, and to that end stay alert with all perseverance and petition concerning all of the saints (Ephesians 6:18).

Together with this, hear the words of Christ to His disciples:

> Watch and pray or you will enter into temptation. The spirit is willing but the flesh is weak (Matthew 26:41).

The best intentions will fail (as Paul emphatically affirmed in Romans 7) when carried out in our own strength, apart from the Spirit. Jesus faced the temptations before Him successfully and defeated the evil one, whereas the disciples fell apart in the hour of trial. Why? Jesus prayed before facing the evil one; they went to sleep.

Of Paul's words in Ephesians 6:18 Hendriksen says:

> In his own power the soldier can do nothing against so great a foe. Hence, as he puts on each piece of his armor and as he makes use of it in the battle, he must pray for God's blessing.[1]

Prayer is not a part of the equipment per se but is the dynamic that makes the use of the equipment profitable. That is so because prayer is the means by which the Christian warrior calls on the Spirit for assistance. Therefore to stride out to battle alone, armed with all the defensive equipment mentioned in Ephesians 6 and brandishing the one offensive element (the Sword of the Spirit), is to court disaster. That is why in both the Matthew passage and the Ephesians one there is a warning to be alert—to be neither negligent nor careless about the matter of prayer. Your best intentions will come to nothing if you depend upon your weak self to win the battle; indeed, it is more than likely that you will end up fighting the very flesh itself!

In Sermon 18 from the book of 2 Timothy (the book he calls his favorite) John Calvin said:

> Therefore we must pray to God that he would strengthen us from day to day, until he takes us out of this world; and let us not think through our own virtue and moving to get mastery over our wicked affections. It is God that must give us that victory.[2]

The prayer of the Christian soldier must be "in" or "by" the Spirit. Jude speaks in the same vein: "Praying by the Holy Spirit" (verse 20). It is important to have the Spirit's aid in *praying* as well as in the battle itself. It is precisely this aid that Paul says the Spirit gives His own, whose prayers so often falter and are incoherent and unintelligent (cf. Romans 8:26,27). So it becomes obvious that the statement in Galatians 5:17 (in which Paul sets up the flesh and the Spirit in opposition to each other, virtually ignoring the believer himself) is indeed the truth. The believer is not really ignored, but the battle is the Lord's; wisdom and strength, at all points, come from Him. Spurgeon was quite right when he said, "All our strength lies in prayer."[3] But also learn this: If God provides for all aspects of the battle, including the very prayer with which you call on Him for provision, then make no mistake—there is no excuse for failure. You cannot even plead that you do not know how to pray!

Prayer is a resource that Satan doesn't possess, and the flesh knows nothing of it. Yet it is yours—a powerful asset which the Lord warns you not to neglect. Of course faithful prayer is difficult, as the disciples discovered and as we all know. And right here many battles are lost. People who know the Word, whose minds are fixed on the right goals and who want to win the war within, nevertheless fail because they do not pray.

Because Jesus knew our proclivity to fail, He went to great lengths to teach us about prayer, including in the Lord's Prayer this important soldier's petition: "Don't bring us into testing, but rather, rescue us from the evil one" (Matthew 6:13). Through parables He urged us to pray. About one of these Luke says, "Then He told them a parable illustrating the need to keep praying and not to give up" (Luke 18:1). Much in the Psalms has to do with prayer in war. Clearly prayer is a vital condition of successful warfare. You do not fight the same way when you pray as when you do not.

Faith

Without faith it is impossible to please God. Moreover, faith is the shield that protects us from assaults of the evil one and our flesh. Faith is an essential piece of a fighting man's equipment (Ephesians 6:16). Of course, every Christian has *saving faith.* But taking *the shield of faith* is a continuing, ongoing, deepening process by which a believer puts himself more and more into his Father's hands, asking Him to guide and direct His life. Such faith eagerly welcomes God's will in His Word, whatever it may be. It can be seen in the willingness to suffer anything for His sake, to endure whatever He wills, and to obey whenever He calls—because He is right.

Phillips Brooks once preached an entire sermon on the fact that truth becomes powerful only when it passes through faith. His text was Hebrews 4:2, where the writer of Hebrews says that the Word did not profit those who heard because it was "not mixed with faith." The same could be said for prayer: We must pray in faith (James 1:6) or our prayers will not be heard. But faith is crucial to power, as Brooks points out, because, until mixed with faith, the Word is inert. He writes:

> Truth and a soul that is ready for truth
> meet like the fuel and the flame.[4]

He laments those "pathetic sights," found everywhere, in which "possibility and failure meet."[5] By this he means people with ideas, with potential, who have always been "on the brink of doing,"[6] but never actually produce. There is but one reason: lack of faith.

Brad lacks both faith and prayer. That is why he has gone so far as to compromise himself and now finds himself teetering on the edge of disaster. Without going into the facts so fully as we did with the case of Mildred, think for a moment about Brad.

His wife is giving him a hard time. She neglects him, makes fun of his new faith, tempts him to sexual sin. What is his response? Self-pity, indulgence in pornography, sinful fantasizing, and contemplation of outright adultery. Surely what he needs is the shield of faith to quench the fiery darts that have been hurled at him! He has also become lax in prayer, and so the enemy has gained several beachheads in his life and is advancing at a steady pace.

What Christian soldier fighting for his country can act that way? When he is in battle, far away from home for long periods of time, is a married man allowed to satisfy his sexual desires with prostitutes? Certainly not. Can he restrain himself? Certainly. Thousands of Christian men who have gone to war will testify that they have. So can Brad. He too is at war. "But the temptations are so great," he pleads. They are great when one is fighting in a foreign land too. That's war! Brad has never learned to endure his "share of suffering as a good soldier of Christ Jesus" (2 Timothy 2:3).

Brad's main problem is that he lacks faith. He does not really believe that God will work things out. He doubts the battle plans of his Commander-in-Chief. He needs a good dose of 1 Corinthians 10:13 and Romans 8:28. The Word, mixed with faith, will provide power to overcome. Right now there is little power and much defeat because there is little faith. John says, "This is what defeats the world: our faith" (1 John 5:4).

But how will Brad acquire the faith he lacks? By reading the Word prayerfully. Instead of indulging in pornography and movies, and spending time fantasizing, he should devote those wasted hours to an

intensive study of the faith-strengthening Word. ✓
Faith comes by hearing and hearing through the
Word of Christ; for too long Brad has been listening
to the wrong voices.

Moreover, as with any soldier on the battlefield,
there is little time to feel sorry for one's self when he
is busily fighting. In faithfully following his God-
given directives, Brad will be so occupied that he
will have neither the time nor the energy to fulfill
the desires of the flesh. That is what "walking in the
Spirit" means: walking according to the will of the
Spirit as revealed in His Word. Surely sitting on the
sidelines, whining and feeling sorry for one's self, is
not walking in the Spirit.

If Brad will put on the armor, move out into the
fray, and take on the enemy, all the while prayerfully
trusting God's Word and Spirit, he will soon discover the power of God at work in his life. Calvin
says:

> ... we cannot serve God, but Satan will
> resist us, and we must fight against the
> assaults which he will make against us ...
> we need not go out of ourselves to know
> what wars mean.[7]

As a man of power—winning the war within by
faith mixed with truth rather than appearing as a
beaten, simpering wimp—Brad may have more
appeal to his wife. Surely if he is ever to take her
captive for Christ, he must first succeed in winning
the war within himself.

How about you? How is the battle going? Are you
losing the war because of deficiencies in prayer
and faith? Examine yourself carefully. Is the flesh

advancing, taking control of large portions of your life, or have you got it on the run? It will always be one or the other; there is no armistice or even temporary cease-fire in this war. Identify the enemy, call on the Spirit to help you, and fight him with all the resources that God has made available to you. As you do this, you will soon turn your present battle into victory!

10

Calling In Reinforcements

The old saying "each barrel stands on its own bottom" is a lie; it does not. From the day you first opened your mouth to breathe until the day you expire, you are dependent on others. Life is dependency. You must depend on God: In Him you "live and move and have your being" (Acts 17:28 KJV). You depended on your parents to feed, protect, and raise you. You depend on farmers for the food you eat and on a legion of unseen faces to provide electricity, water, transportation, and numberless other services necessary for you to make your living and to carry on your modern mode of existence. If anything characterizes you, it is the word *dependent*.

Why then do we hear such a disparagement of the web of interdependency on which we all find ourselves crawling? What shall we say, for example, of the "self-made man"? He is a fiction. There never was such a creature. God didn't make people that way. Someone has said, "There is no smaller package than a person all wrapped up in himself." The so-called self-made man is simply an ingrate! He is a proud, ungrateful wretch who fails to acknowledge either the help of God or that of multitudes of other people who have helped him in any number of ways. Many a battle has been lost by those who think they are self-sufficient!

When You Have
Difficulty Fighting Alone

Not every Christian at every point in his life is able to engage successfully in the hand-to-hand combat that the war within requires. He finds himself going down under the enemy's sword. Yet many Christians are too proud to call for help. A woman said today, "I'm not a member of the church—I don't need it!" She is wrong. Time will tell. God provided not only the Holy Spirit—who, of course, is the ultimate Helper—but the church, through which the Spirit often provides such help. After all, the Spirit is not at work in you alone. He is at work in the lives of other Christians all over the world. And he has been at work in the lives of many in past years too.

Every preacher worth his salt knows this. That is why he studies commentaries and books by other preachers. He knows that the Spirit gave insight into the meaning of biblical passages to others before him, and he is unwilling to deprive himself or his congregation of such insight. He knows also that, in the present, God has provided elders to assist him in his task. And he knows that Christ's work is properly carried on by every member of the body (Ephesians 4:11,12). Only foolish preachers fail to work closely with other Christians, calling on them to fight side by side as he leads them into the Lord's battles.

Mildred found the help of other Christians invaluable. While at first she seemingly made the decision to return home on her own, even then it was because of the ministry of others in the past who had taught her in church, in her youth group, and in the church school. The Spirit of God was active within her, helping her to recall the words of Scripture taught in years past, and helping her to apply them to her current situation. Doubtless the providence of God was at work as well, arranging for Rob to disclose his real attitudes, and even (in a taunt intended for anything but good) to suggest the proper course of action.

Indeed, in every step of Mildred's pathway back to God she was dependent upon the help of others. Later her parents, the pastor (as he counseled), the congregation, and the many women who spent time with Mildred over the days of her pregnancy all contributed to her reclamation. We are truly dependent people. There is no such thing as a "lone wolf" Christian, or, as the Germans (thinking of its lonely voyages) say, a "submarine Christian."

You too may be in need of help. It is not wrong for you to ask for it. Indeed, you could do nothing more important if you find yourself in the thick of the battle, losing your fight with the flesh. Call; call now! Call for reinforcements. Don't wait until you have lost the battle. Don't wait till someone else must call for the stretcher-bearers. Call for others to stand beside you and help you, so that you may win the battle for the sake of Jesus Christ.

Did you notice those last words: "for the sake of Jesus Christ"? Yes, that should overcome your reluctance to seek help. You are not merely fighting a battle of your own; this is the *Lord's* battle, and it is to be won for His glory. How dare you assume that this battle is yours? Who do you think you are? How can you say, "It's my business whether I win or lose?" How can you tell others who want to help you to "mind their own business"? Fighting the Lord's battles *is the business of the whole church.*

All Christians have a stake in one another because we are all in the Lord's army. There are no private battles. If you are engaged in private battles, you are fighting the wrong battles in life. You are probably fighting against one of your brothers in the Lord whom you ought to be helping rather than fighting.

So don't hesitate to call in the reinforcements when you find yourself in trouble.

Accepting Help

✓ Every Christian is required to come to the assistance of another whenever he discovers him losing the battle. Paul wrote:

> Bear one another's burdens and so fulfill Christ's law (Galatians 6:2).

This command was given in the context of assisting those who had become entangled in some sin from which they were not extracting themselves (Galatians 6:1). In other words, it is a command to help a brother who is losing, to turn the tide of battle. God orders you in love to move into the fray alongside any brother whom you discover being overcome by the enemy. Your aim must be to "restore" him to his place of usefulness, so that now helped, healed, and hearty in the faith he can carry his own share of the load (Galatians 6:5). How often have you obeyed that command? Or do you hesitate to move in to help others in such circumstances? If so, it is time you began to appreciate the dependency which we all have upon one another in the Lord's work. There is ample help available to show you how to obey this command if you are hesitant because of lack of knowledge.[1]

But here I mainly want to mention the unwillingness to accept help that is found among many defeated believers. Due to foolish pride, there are Christians today who lose battles with the flesh, not because there is no help available but because they will not avail themselves of it. That is unconscionable; the battle is not yours but the Lord's. How dare you—if you are a defeated Christian—refuse help? God has commanded others to help you, and He commands *you* to receive such help.

There are those who plead that they have the Holy Spirit to help them. Yes, but the Spirit often works through the ministry of His Word by other Christians. Christ Himself gave the gift of teachers to His church. He also provided encouragers and helpers of all sorts (Ephesians 4:11; Romans 12:6-8). To fail to avail yourself of these provisions, and to haughtily maintain that you would rather fight by using your own resources alone, is in effect to say that Christ did not know what He was doing when He set up His church. The only other possible explanation is that you think you are an exception, above needing help from others, so that Christ's provisions which are so important for other Christians are unnecessary for you. Either way, the problem is pride.

Many battles with the flesh are lost because of pride: pride that silences the lips of the one who is fighting and losing because of the embarrassment of admitting it, and pride of the one who is offered help and refuses it. The important point to emphasize is simply this: *You are fighting for Christ in His army.* When He tells you to give or receive help, those are orders. You are not the Commander-in-Chief; *He* is. You must obey orders, like them or not, and embarrassed or not. After all, what is embarrassment? It is the clearest evidence of pride. When you are embarrassed, it is because whatever the task, you think you ought to be able to accomplish it on your own, and are embarrassed when you find that you can't.

There are many battles that cannot be fought alone. That is why Christ has provided help in His church and ordered His troops to help one another in fighting them. We tell people who are hesitant to come for help (whether it is for counseling about some complex situation or for simple encouragement and direction): "As soon as you feel yourself sinking, and know that your efforts to extricate yourself are useless, shout for help. Don't wait until the quicksand gets up around your neck. It's always a lot harder on everyone when all we can get hold of is an ear!"

Are you having troubles in your marriage? Are you losing a battle with lust? With lying? With thievery? With anger or bitterness? With discouragement? Do the forces of evil seem to be storming the citadel of your soul in some other way? Then call for reinforcements. Don't wait. You need additional forces right now!

Take an example or two. Yesterday a woman asked on the phone whether she ought to seek forgiveness from another person when she hasn't the faintest idea how she might have offended him. She was right to seek help rather than move ahead on poor, unbiblical advice. Probably she should have turned to her pastor instead of me to discover that if someone is angry she is obligated to go and try to be reconciled with him (Matthew 5:23,24), even as it was the obligation of the other person to go and confront her with the alleged wrong (Matthew 18:15ff.; Luke 17:3ff.). But at any rate she was willing to admit her ignorance and to seek help in order to learn how best to win the battle. Just for a little while I drew near and fought with her in order to help her overcome the battle.

On my desk lies a letter that arrived today. It contains several requests, one of which is for me to come and mediate between a pastor and some estranged members. They are all losing their battles. But this pastor, unlike many, is willing to admit he needs reinforcements. Even pastors at times need help. His is an independent church. There is no presbytery or other body of men to whom he can appeal. I have had an acquaintance with the congregation and with him in the past, so now I am being asked to bring in the reinforcements. To the best of my ability, God giving me strength, I will do so.*

The Holy Spirit works through His Word, as we have seen. But the Word, as I said above, is often the ✓ Word *ministered*. What does that mean? Remember the words of the apostles in Acts 6:4: "...we will continue to devote ourselves to prayer and the ministry of the Word." The word "ministry" means "service," just as the word "minister" means "servant." God appointed pastor-teachers to serve His Word. Almost as waiters serving a table, the minister

---

* Two days later I write this footnote: Today I received a phone call from the elder of an independent congregation, asking me to mediate a dispute between their pastor and the board of elders. Perhaps Christians, at last, have begun to seek help rather than allow matters to deteriorate further.

of the Word is to offer the healthy truths of Scripture to those who are in need of them. In so doing it is his task to find, explain, and apply those truths that fit the circumstances of those to whom he ministers.

The minister of the Word helps both by preaching the Word and by the individual ministry of the Word which we would call counseling (Acts 20:20; Colossians 1:28). Either way, it is the same Word generally proclaimed (or, in counseling, applied more particularly) that must be ministered. It is the Word of God through which the Holy Spirit encourages, guides, and strengthens. Sometimes the more casual help of fellow believers is what makes all the difference:

> Instead, encourage one another every day...so that none of you will become hardened by sin's deceiving way (Hebrews 3:13).

That is why it is important for every believer to obey the command found later on in the same book not to

> abandon our practice of meeting together, as some are in the habit of doing (Hebrews 10:25a),

since

> we must encourage each other, and all the more as you see the day drawing near (Hebrews 10:25b).

Much of such help will be preventative, if utilized properly. Some will be remedial. But in either case, close and personal ties with the church must be cultivated and maintained so that whatever the need for help, the channels for giving help, and for asking and receiving help, may be kept clear.

11

Defeat

Defeat! It's not a pleasant word, is it? Yet some of the greatest men in biblical history—Moses, Abraham, David, Solomon, Peter—knew defeat and conquered it! What was their secret?

In the war within you will experience defeat whenever you win or lose a battle. That is because in either case one side or the other within you will lose. In every decisive battle either your "mind" or your "flesh" (Romans 7:25) will go down in defeat. When you lose the battle to the flesh, you first experience the exultation of victory, only to be followed in time by the bitterness of defeat leading to repentance. You indulge in the pleasure of some sin, reveling in your seeming freedom and the temporary delights it provides (Hebrews 11:25b), only to end in despair because you have offended the Lord and grieved His Spirit. But the peculiar fact is that when the Spirit enables you to triumph over the flesh, you know the glories of lasting victory!

But it is the triumph of the flesh over your mind (inner person) about which I wish to think with you in this chapter. Defeat can be discouraging. Indeed, the evil one would like nothing better than to convince you to give up the war in despair, allowing yourself to be taken captive by the flesh.

But that is precisely what you must not allow to happen. God has not only made it possible to defeat the flesh (Luther says that because of Christ's work on the cross "...you can now readily resist sin";[1] cf. 1 Peter 4:2), but has also made provision for helping you emerge from defeat as a victor in the end (cf. James 5:19,20). You will notice in the passage just cited that James, no less than Paul (Galatians 6:1), expects Christians to help one another turn defeat into victory.

But we have described mutual ministry in the last chapter in some detail. Now I want to think about the consequences of defeat, not so much in terms of its ultimate effects or how others may intervene to extricate one from it, but defeat as it affects the one who loses a battle. What can he do about it?

The Loss Is Temporary

You know that in spite of some defeat you have just suffered, along with similar defeat in the lives of thousands of other Christians all over the world, ultimately Christ will win the cosmic war, the global war, and even the personal war within you. You are on the winning side. That should not make you careless, as if what you do is not all that important, but rather it should encourage you to get up, repair the damage, and go forth again—this time to victory! You are fighting a war that, in Christ, you know you can win. If you are losing battles, it is only your fault. All the provisions for winning are yours. You must learn to use them!

Ultimately, if you are really God's child, He will take you to Himself, at last removing all sin from you as that degraded body (whose members are habitu-ated to do evil—Philippians 3:21) will be laid aside, to be transformed in time into a new and glorious body that no longer fights against you. Instead, it will become totally cooperative, desiring and learn-ing to desire only those ways that please the Lord. Think of it—a body (which of course includes the brain, since the body is everything that goes into the ground and rots) fully submissive to the leading of the Spirit!

Defeat, rather than causing you despair, should cause you to long for that day and encourage you to live now as close to the reality of it as possible. You have the potential in the Spirit and the Word to begin to experience victories even now! Luther, that old veteran in the wars of the Lord, says that Scrip-ture

> ... teaches how to crush the head of the serpent and to slay the evil.[2]

According to him, the Christian

> is furnished with power to crush the ser-pent's head ... also power to constantly crucify his flesh.[3]

And he insisted that the Holy Spirit

> gives help and strength by means of which they [believers] can resist and put sin to death.[4]

Notice that it is the Christian, using the Scrip-tures in the power of the Spirit, to which Luther points. There is no other combination that will win battles.

Recouping

The second fact of which you should be aware is that you can recoup from failure. The passage from James 5:19,20 commends those who "bring back" sinning believers "who err from the truth" and thereby "cover a multitude of sins." This means that defeat can be turned into triumph for the Lord.

You do not need to go on falling into the same sins time and time again. You can defeat the body's ways, rehabituating it to operate in ways that please God. Christ broke the power that sin held over you (Romans 6:6). Sin need no longer reign in your members (Romans 6:12).

In 2 Timothy 3:16 Paul says that one of the four functions of the Scriptures in the life of the believer, as the Spirit uses them to effect change, is "correction." The Greek word means "to stand up straight again." The flesh may knock you flat, and the convicting power of the Bible may only seem to intensify your problems (by seeming to kick you when you are down), but the Scriptures never leave you there. They humble you in order to show you the error of your ways and bring you to repentance before God, but then they pick you up, dust you off, turn you around, show you the way out of your sin, and tell you what to do to avoid it in the future. You *can* change, and one of the principal ways that God uses to bring change to rebellious children is through defeat.[5]

Third, you must recognize that in the long run defeat may be the path to victory.

After World War I, Germany was forced by the treaty that ended hostilities to destroy most of its weapons, war equipment, and ammunition. But as a result, when World War II began, the Germans were the only national power equipped with modern equipment and fresh ammunition. This is one reason for their rapid defeat of Poland, the Low Countries, and France. The Allies lost much ground at the outset because, not being forced to destroy their outmoded equipment, they depended on outdated stock that was no match for the new German material. They were plagued with shells that didn't explode, planes that were too slow, tanks that were outclassed, and a lack of antitank equipment and mines of types that the enemy possessed in abundance. The terms of the German defeat actually gave them the opportunity to take advantage of change, a fact that was all too apparent at the outset of the next war.

Moreover, during the years between the two world wars the German military studied carefully the reasons for their previous defeat, and, long before Hitler came to power, had developed new strategies and tactics based on what they had learned.

What I am saying is simply this: Often it takes a resounding defeat to convince you of your deficiencies, to crush your pride and sense of self-sufficiency, and to awaken you to God's new possibilities for the future. Defeat can be the sharpest teaching tool in the Spirit's kit.

That is in part what Jesus was talking about when He urged us to pluck out the eye or cut off the hand or foot that sins, even if it is the right (most important) one. This teaching about radical amputation, often repeated in different contexts in the Gospels, means 1) study how you fell into sin, 2) take preventative action (radical, if necessary) to make yourself aware of any future drift into that sin in the future, and 3) take action that will make it difficult to sin that way again.

If you must hop over to the place of sin on your remaining foot (having amputated the other) you cannot very easily fall into the sin unawares, since one characteristic of habit is that it is unconscious and automatic. Nor will you be able to actually perform the act of sin with the bloody stump that is left after amputating the hand that previously did the deed. You will make it difficult for yourself to sin again in the future.

Do nothing, letting the flesh alone, and it will soon have its way. Take no precautions against it and you will find it taking over. We often put ourselves in temptation's way, asking for trouble by failing to follow Jesus' clear-cut directions. That too is sin, because Jesus has commanded us to take radical action.

Of course, Jesus doesn't want you to maim your body; He is using a powerful figure of speech to drive home the urgency of taking strong preventive measures to assure against future failure. Like Germany, you must learn from your defeat.

Correction, however, must be followed by rehabituation of the body, in which it learns to automatically, unconsciously, comfortably, and skillfully (the four characteristics of habit) respond according to those biblical alternatives that please God. It is not enough to "put off" the old ways; they must be *replaced* by God's new ways which the Spirit enables you to "put on" by rehabituating the body to desire and perform them (cf. Ephesians 4; Colossians 3).

Indeed, Brooks speaks of the futility of simply telling someone to break with his sinful ways:

> And now what has the New Testament, what has Christianity, what has Christ to say to that hot and rebellious soul? Anything? ... It seems to me I can see Christ approach that man. ... I do not hear Him use such words of utter and unsparing rebuke as I have many a time heard lavished on youthful dissipation, and yet His face is sadder over that poor boy's wandering than the father's or mother's face ever grew. "My brother," I can hear Him say, "you are not wholly wrong. Nay, at the bottom you are right. Self-mortification, self-sacrifice, is not the first or final law of life. You are right when you think that these appetites and passions were not put into you merely to be killed, and that the virtue which only comes by their restraint is a poor, colorless, and feeble thing. You are right in thinking that not to restrain yourself and to refrain from doing, but to utter yourself, to act, to do, is the purpose of your being in the world. Only, my brother, this is not the self you are to utter, these are not the acts you are to do. There is a part of you made to think deeply, made to feel nobly, made to be charitable and chivalric, made to worship, to pity, and to love. You are not uttering yourself while you keep that better self in chains and only let these lower passions free. Let me renew those nobler powers, and then believe with all your heart and might that

to send out those powers into the intensest exercise is the one worthy purpose of your life. Then these passions, which you are indulging because you cannot believe that you were meant to give your whole life up to bridling them, will need no forcible bridling, and yet, owning their masters in the higher powers which come out to act, they will be content to serve them. You will not fulfill your passions any longer, but the reason will not be that you have resumed the weary guard over your passions which you tried to keep of old. It will be that you have given yourself up so utterly to the seeking after holiness that these lower passions have lost their hold upon you. You will not so much have crushed the carnal as embraced the spiritual. I shall have made you free. You will be walking in the Spirit, and so will not fulfill the lusts of the flesh."[6]

You may or may not agree with all that Brooks has said, or the way he says it, but don't fail to miss this point: Brooks is saying that *there must be no mere negativism.* It is not enough to attempt to break the habits of the past without replacing them; you must not empty the house of undesirable guests without renting it to desirable ones. He is saying, in addition, that the way to drive out the old is to replace it with the new. He is saying that the way to defeat the old sinful manner of life is to fall in love with a new and finer one. He is saying that to draw away allegiance from the flesh you must develop a greater allegiance to Christ. No soldier fights more nobly than the soldier who fights for those he loves. Brooks is speaking of what Chalmers called "the expulsive power of a new affection."

So you see that defeat, rightly handled, need not always end as a tragedy.

Let's take Brad, for example. Much of what Brooks had to say could be applied to him. If challenged properly to see that he had been fighting wrongly by rationalizing sin and defeat rather than recognizing it for what it is, even at this late date Brad could turn his failure into success, his defeat into triumph—perhaps even a triumph that could lead his wife into submission to Christ and her husband! At any rate, if he learns from his defeats he will gain a position of strength, so that in the future, regardless of what happens, he will be able to *stand* (Ephesians 6:13,14) rather than fall.

You too may be defeated. But look up—your redemption draws near (Luke 21:28). You need suffer only a little while (1 Peter 5:10). You *can* overcome the sin that now so easily besets you. If you don't know how to change, how to handle future temptation, call in reinforcements. There are others who can point you to biblical answers, and there are books (a number of which I have footnoted throughout this volume) that can assist you. Take advantage of both.

You need no longer be defeated. God expects you to recoup. In amazement He says to defeated, backsliding Israel:

> When men fall, do they not rise again? If one turns away, does he not come back? Why then is this people of Jerusalem turned away in perpetual backsliding (Jeremiah 8:4,5 Berkeley).

It is the way with our Savior to turn tragedy into triumph. His Spirit can do the same for you—believe it! Stop sulking, lay aside that anger, leave behind your despair—or whatever seems to be hindering you—and learn from your defeat. Then you will discover that "the God of peace will soon crush Satan under your feet" (Romans 16:20).

12

Hindrances

Falling into sin is always *your* fault. That is clear from the facts we have been studying. God has freed you from the dominion of sin, has placed the Holy Spirit within you to enable you to understand the Bible and follow it, and has given you great encouragements through His promises to strengthen you. Therefore, when I talk about hindrances I want to make it very plain from the outset that what I have in mind are just hindrances, and nothing more. The martyrs always stand out as unimpeachable examples of the fact that no one else can make you sin.

I shall be talking about three principal obstacles that you will find in the way when you fight the war within. They are impediments to progress, it is true, but they are not absolute, immovable, or impenetrable. Overcoming these hindrances is a significant part of fighting the war within. The fact to be grasped before going further is that, no matter how difficult that task may be, in Christ you have all you need in order to overcome.

When an enemy retreats, he often blows up the bridges behind him. That is done in order to impede the progress of the army pursuing him. Certainly, rivers without bridges are serious hindrances to tanks and infantry, but they are not insurmountable. We have seen how armies carry specially trained troops that, within a few hours, can build temporary bridges across great rivers for their troops to pass over. Obstacles to winning the war within that are put there by the world, the flesh, and the devil *must be overcome*. But to do so requires persistence, faith, and courage.

The discussion that follows is concerned only with the most common obstacles that the flesh puts in your way. In no sense is the list exhaustive. You may find that you have relatively few difficulties with one or more of these problems while struggling fiercely with matters I have not mentioned. It is true that there are problems peculiar to each of us, but in addition we all seem to have some problems in common. It is these common problems that I wish to consider.

Entangling One's Self

This is a problem common enough for Paul to warn Timothy about:

> A soldier avoids becoming involved in everyday business activities so that he may please the one who enlisted him (2 Timothy 2:4).

Can't you see someone out on the battlefield, trying to fight the enemy while making and receiving long-distance phone calls from a mobile phone unit in touch with his place of business at home? He is trying to conduct business while carrying on the Lord's battles! The very picture which this conjures up in the mind is absurd. Paul's words are another way of saying "You cannot serve two masters." You must concentrate on the battle. When you fight, you must throw all your energies into the fray; you dare not dissipate them by spreading them over other interests and concerns.

In other words, winning the war within, just as winning wars without, demands wholehearted commitment.

There are always tempting sidetracks that appear along the course of battle, to lure you from the unpleasantness that lies ahead. It is easy to think of skirmishes about esoteric doctrinal issues, speculative matters, questionable activities, and so forth as the real battle, when all they turn out to be are the enemy's diversionary tactics designed to hinder your progress. But you must be careful here. True issues over doctrine are important; a correct understanding of the teachings of Scripture is essential for proper Christian living. You will never win battles in the war within apart from the application of truth to life.

But there is a sort of "irreligious chatter" that "will eat like gangrene" (2 Timothy 2:16,17), will tear down "those who listen" (verse 14), and will lead to "even more ungodliness" (verse 16). Compare especially 2 Timothy 2:23: "But avoid foolish and undisciplined speculations, knowing that they breed battles." There is a kind of preoccupation about speculative matters (particularly those that fall into the category of those things that God has not chosen to reveal to us—Deuteronomy 29:29) that itself becomes the occasion for fights with others ("breeds battles"). Becoming involved in these only hampers one as he tries to fight battles within that at the moment may be his number one priority.

It is easy to win battles on the outside, slaying heresy wherever it is found, while continuously losing battles within. One wonders at times about those who are always hunting heresy, with never anything positive to say about the truth. If you find someone whose "ministry" is wholly negative, you will almost always find a person whose own personal battles are being lost. The negative must indeed be exposed and the battles with error must indeed be fought, but the reason must always be the glory of the Lord and the welfare of His church. And one must always be sure that his own life is up to snuff when he ventures out into the battlefield to attack sin in other people. His eye must be free from the log before he can remove the speck from others. Then, too, his motives must be right. The positive outlook—honoring God and building up His work (not merely tearing down the enemy's strongholds)— must always dominate. Unfortunately, some Christians feel more at home with the wrecking crew than with the construction gang.

Whatever "entangles" a person is anything that distracts his attention from essential battles within. In short, it is a hindrance that must be eliminated. It is the next battle.

Hindrances have a way of diverting attention and dissipating energies. That is their danger. I have mentioned just one example, but there are many others. Indeed, almost anything—even those things that are right and good (like the business affairs of this life mentioned by Paul)—may become hindrances when fighting a battle. A soldier finds that his ordinary, peacetime course of life must be laid aside for another course during war. War means new objectives, new routines, and new priorities. That is the kind of wholehearted effort which the Lord expects of you when fighting His battles.

It is interesting to note how Paul made use of the current practice in recruiting armies during his time to drive home the motive which every Christian should have when fighting for the Lord: "that he may please the one who enlisted him." In those days armies were recruited mostly by famous generals who called their men to personal allegiance. They fought for Alexander the Great, for example, as only his soldiers could, because they so greatly admired him and wanted him to win his battles. No wonder he wept at the age of 30 because he had "no more worlds to conquer"!

Jesus Christ, the Lord, enlisted you! That is the unspoken but nonetheless clear implication of Paul's words. You must not allow anything to diminish your wholehearted effort to fight the war within so that the Lord, by His Spirit, may reign supreme. You must fight with the sole aim of pleasing Him, regardless of the cost to yourself. The Lord expects your full support whenever He strides forth into battle, whether it be in the world, the church, or your heart. Battles fought in any other way, even though apparently won, are not really won at all because they are carried on with one eye on the Lord and another on our own interests. That is what must be avoided at all costs.

Giving Up

There are those who become weary in well-doing. Paul says, "Don't!" Here are his words: "Don't get tired of doing what is good [fine]; for at the right time we shall reap if we don't slacken" (Galatians 6:9). One way of doing good (the word here is not "good" as opposed to "evil," but that which is *fine* as over against that which is shoddy) is to persevere in battle. Too many Christians start off well but finish poorly because at some point when the battle seems to be going against them, they quit. So they make a shoddy mess of it.

The figure of "reaping" in time is not a military one, though the truth expressed by it certainly is. If you endure, hanging in there when the going gets tough and continuing to fight regardless of the hindrances and obstacles that the flesh may fling in your way, in time (God's time) *you will win.*

But we do not have to look to a figure from farming to understand this truth. In 2 Timothy 2:3 the Lord commands: "Endure your share of suffering as a good soldier of Jesus Christ." Here, spelling out who it is that enlisted you, Paul expressed the Lord's wishes: "*endure*"; indeed, "endure your share of *suffering.*"

Wars are no fun. They can grow old quickly. They sap one's energies and often tax him to the uttermost. And there is suffering to be *endured.* Christ's "good" (again, the word is "fine" or "properly fighting") soldiers are prepared for the long haul, no matter how severe the battle grows. They consider it their job to bear a certain amount of the suffering that wars occasion, and they are ready to bear it for their Lord's sake. They remember the suffering that He bore for them!

To fight against sin in your life will not be a pleasant task. It hurts to give up cherished ways. Sin does not surrender easily; it will put up a strong fight.

Counselees who are struggling to overcome some sin often give up and go back to their old ways. One of the things that good, biblical counselors always warn them about is the fact that they must hang in there when the going gets tough, as it usually does. While they hold out all the hope that there is in Christ Jesus, they make it clear that there are no automatic or magical roads to success.

It is because people don't want to endure prolonged battles with the flesh, and instead desire quicker, less painful ways of eliminating sin, that they invent their own methods for doing so. One popular idea is to call on "experts" to cast out demons of envy, anger, lust, etc. These so-called "deliverance" ministries are substitutes for the often long, wearisome, painful wars to which you were called as a Christian. Don't be fooled by such "ministries." If exorcism of sin, in the form of such "labeled" demons, were truly God's way of deliverance from the flesh, then the New Testament would exhort you to go to your pastor (or some other "expert") to have demons cast out. However, there is not even a whisper of any such command in the Bible. If you don't believe me, check it out for yourself.

On the other hand, there is command after command urging you to persevere, endure, and suffer for Christ's sake. Indeed, one of the ways to distinguish a Christian from those who make a false profession of faith is that "whoever endures to the end will be saved" (Matthew 10:22b). The branches that claimed to be in the vine but do not "remain" in Christ never had any vital connection with Him in the first place and will be burned (John 15:6). A true

Christian endures hardship as a good soldier of Jesus Christ.

The battle is not pleasant. Luther once wrote:

> They must fight against it [the flesh] as long as they live, at the cost of much pain and weariness.[1]

But how does one endure? We could do no better than to turn to Paul's words on the subject. After all, if there ever was a good soldier of Christ, who gave us an example of untiring endurance, it was he. I will not take the space here to quote the two extensive catalogs of his sufferings found in 2 Corinthians 6:4-10 and 11:23-29, but I do commend them to you to read whenever you are feeling sorry for yourself. They are particularly useful whenever you are tempted to give up. Here is a man who endured far more than most of us will ever even approach. Yet he didn't give up. Listen to his testimony:

> We are afflicted in all sorts of ways, but not crushed; perplexed, but not given to despair (2 Corinthians 4:8).

At the beginning of the same chapter he wrote:

> Therefore, since we have this service to perform as the result of mercy, we don't give up (verse 1).

How was it that Paul was able to persevere to the end in spite of the fury of the battle that raged around him?

Two things are apparent in the chapter. First, Paul knew that God had been gracious to him, and he was grateful for it. He had been saved and had been given a ministry to perform "as the result of mercy." He certainly did not deserve to serve the living God as His apostle. He had been a murderer and a persecutor of the faith which he now preached. No man ever understood grace more profoundly than the apostle Paul, who experienced so much grace himself. He had been given a ministry, and he would perform it until the Lord told him to stop. *Man* could not stop him, unless God so decreed. It was not *his* business to decide when to stop fighting. That was all in the Lord's hands; as a good soldier he would simply continue to obey the orders of the One who called him until such a time as they were changed.

So the first important factor to remember is that you must fight out of *gratitude.* No other motive is powerful enough to enable you to endure. God has saved you and called you to fight in His cause. You must get this life of yours in shape for His service by winning the war within. That is His command, and He has never withdrawn the order. So, whether you feel like it or not, don't give up. Certainly, when Paul was left for dead in a heap of rocks at Lystra he felt like giving up—but he didn't. God had not withdrawn His orders. You will feel like giving up too, but you may not. Indeed, as you focus on the mercy and the grace of God shown to you, you will not want to quit.

Paul did not give up because he was fighting out of the right motive. But there is a second reason why Paul did not give up:

> As a result, we do not give up, even though
> our outer person is decaying, because [on
> the other hand] our inner person is being
> renewed daily (2 Corinthians 4:16).

Paul was literally falling apart physically, but within—just where resources are needed so badly to fight a war "within"—he was being "renewed daily." Few things are more important to an army on the march than a good supply line. If supplies are cut off, then it is just a matter of time till the men must give up. But there is no reason to fear that this will happen in the Lord's army. The great Commander-in-Chief has seen to it that all the resources you need are readily available to you, if you seek them in the right way. He will never leave you in the lurch.

That fact alone is a great encouragement to keep fighting even in the bitterest battles. You will be reinforced with all the resources needed—as needed. Sometimes we refuse to move out until all the resources are at hand. God nowhere promises that. As you need them (Paul says "daily") you will get them— not before. That is what faith (about which we had a bit to say earlier) is all about. God promises all you need, *when you need it*, to fight the battle successfully. What more could you want than that? But it takes faith to act on His promises. Depending on daily inner supplies rather than on stockpiles of ammunition, rations, etc. at the outset of a battle is a matter of faith.

Going to battle with the flesh, the enemy that has defeated you so often before, is not easy when you see no resources available except those for one day at a time. But to such warfare, Christian, you are called. Don't give up!

Cowardice

If the Lord prepares us for the battle, provides for our every need, and fights the flesh with us, then why don't we fight? Apathy? Yes, that is one reason. And the solution to it is renewed gratitude, as we have seen. Lack of faith? Yes, that is another reason. The solution to that problem is to understand (and depend on) God's promise of daily provision. Then why not fight? One hindrance that looms on the horizon of many Christians is *fear*—fear of the enemy, fear of the new and unknown, fear of what others will say and do if they begin to live according to a new lifestyle.

What is needed is *courage and boldness*. During this Caspar Milquetoast period of the church's existence it is tragic to hear the pampering of Christians that is recommended on radio, in books, and from the pulpit. People are told to be careful not to destroy each other's self-esteem (as if such a thing were possible), to "accept" and "respect" all sorts of opinions (even those that contradict Scripture), and never to condemn a viewpoint as false, but instead tolerate all views (except, of course, the view that is intolerant of falsehood). They are to condemn only sin, never the sinner. Counselors must never counsel *directly* (even though the biblical meaning of counseling is *direction*) but must understand and respect the counselee's views (even when they constitute rebellion against God) and be very careful at all times not to harm sensitive egos.

Accepting and following such unbiblical nonsense turns people into cowards. Eventually they are afraid even of their own shadow, cast by the

flesh! To fight successfully, a soldier must be coura-
geous. Certainly there is a natural fear that makes
one properly cautious and preserves life, but the
fear of man, the fear of self, and the fear of inner
warfare ultimately boils down to just one thing: a
lack of the fear of the Lord!

Luther wrote:

> Spiritual strength is not the strength of
> muscle and bones, it is true courage—
> boldness of heart.[2]

When going forth to fight for the Lord, God told
Joshua:

> Be strong and courageous (Joshua 1:6
> NASB).

In the next verse He repeated:

> Only be strong and very courageous
> (NASB).

After telling Joshua in the rest of verse 7 and the
verse that follows it that he would find his fighting
orders in the Bible, from which he was to veer neither to the right nor to the left (verse 7), but to do all
that is written in it (verse 8), God continued:

> Be strong and courageous! Do not trem-
> ble or be dismayed, for the Lord your God
> is with you wherever you go (verse 9 NASB).

There seems to be no question that the Lord
expects courage from those who fight His battles.
If Joshua needed it, you will too. The preacher's

prayer, found in Acts 4:29, "So now, Lord, take note of their threats and give your slaves all the boldness needed to speak Your word," is a prayer for boldness. The word means "freedom to speak without an encumbering fear of consequences." If you are fearful and unbelieving, this can become a principal hindrance to growth in the conquest of sin in your life.

Because of the flabby condition of so many members of the church today, brought about by the encouragement of an unbiblical self-centeredness, cowardice rather than courage prevails. We are even afraid of ourselves! We are afraid that if we attack the sin within us we will do some harm to our "psyche," or at the very least fail in the assault and thus harm our fragile sense of self-worth!

As a matter of fact the danger lies in an opposite direction. Cowardice places one in jeopardy of hell. Along with murderers, the sexually immoral, liars, idolators (and others), the "cowardly" will be cast into the lake of fire (Revelation 21:8). And note that cowards head this list!

What is the solution? Again, boldness comes from trusting God's promises. He promised two things to Joshua: 1) I will be with you as you fight, no matter where you go; 2) I have given you clear biblical orders and directions for winning the war. Follow them closely, do not improvise, and you will have "good success." The same is true today. Listen to Joel:

> Let all fighting men draw near, let them all go up! . . . Let the weak one say, "I am strong" (Joel 3:9,10 Berkeley).

There are many other hindrances to the successful pursuit of the war within, but these three seem to
be a problem everywhere today. They, along with
anything else that may be peculiarly your problem,
can be overcome. No obstacle, however awesome it
seems, is an obstacle to the Lord. He is the God who
moves mountains. He fights on your side; the Holy
Spirit opposes the flesh. When you avail yourself of
the courage and strength that He provides as you
prayerfully pursue His Word, you will overcome all
obstacles. So if you go on sinning, don't complain
about the obstacles or hindrances in your way, but
instead blame yourself!

13

Maintaining a Military Mentality

Reading a book like this may stir the military sense within you. You may be moved by thinking about God's call to battle, and determine to fight valiantly in His cause, casting down the enemy and driving him from the Spirit's temple. The battle may go well for a while, but sooner or later forces will appear that, if allowed to do so, will siphon off your determination and zeal. In this chapter I shall endeavor to acquaint you with God's way for you to remain an alert, battle-prepared soldier of the Lord Jesus Christ.

There are two passages in 1 Peter that say it all:

> Therefore, buckling the belts of your minds for action, keeping level-headed, set your hope entirely on the grace that will be brought to you at the revelation of Jesus Christ (1 Peter 1:13).

> Therefore, since Christ has suffered in the flesh, arm yourselves also with that thought, because whoever has suffered in the flesh has come to a parting of the ways with sin. As a result, it is now possible to live the remainder of your time in the flesh

no longer following human desires but following God's will (1 Peter 4:1,2).

Both of these passages focus on the thought-life.
The Christian ought to be prepared to move out at
any time. As Calvin says from time to time in his
sermons, a believer must keep one foot lifted, always
ready to go. He will develop the mentality of a
soldier—ready to drop everything to go over the top
at a moment's notice—or he will not. Thought-life,
as Peter implies, is all-important.

Two basic factors are raised by Peter: 1) The
Christian soldier must be mentally prepared to take
action here and now because he is oriented toward
the day when the battle will be over and the victory is
won (1 Peter 1:13); and 2) because Christ came in
the flesh, defeated sin, and released him from the
dominion of sin, the Christian must arm himself
with these great facts as he seeks to live the rest of his
life following Jesus rather than the sinful desires
within. The thought? *Christ has made this possible.*

Two things are basic for the kind of military mentality that Christ expects His troops to maintain at
all times: 1) They must know that the victory is
certain and must therefore be ready and anxious to
go to battle at once, knowing that the sooner the
battles are fought and won, the sooner the troops
will go home (to heaven); and 2) they must always
remember that it is not only possible for them to win
the battles they fight but that they can be "more than
conquerors" through Jesus Christ (Romans 8:37).

These thoughts, distilled and mixed together,
form a mentality of victory. Dispirited troops are
poor fighters. They don't want to fight; they want to
go home. And when they can't do so they are all too

willing to surrender to the enemy when they get the chance. Their minds are on anything and everything else but the battle. They are reluctant to go to battle; they even imagine at times that there is no war. The last thing they look forward to is the next battle. How can they get out of their present predicament with their own skins intact? That is the principal concern on their minds. They know—or at least think they know—that there is no hope. They have given up.

Troops that are winning a war see the bright prospects of victory just ahead. They too look forward to the end of the war, but for a very different reason: They look forward to the spoils of victory. Therefore they are alert, ready, and prepared for battle at all times. They are anxious to get going and bring hostilities to their glorious end. Jesus has promised to pour out His grace upon His own when He is revealed as the Great God and Savior (cf. also Titus 2:13).

The Lord, through the teaching of Peter quoted at the beginning of this chapter, intends among other things to instill high morale among His troops. A fighting force with high morale is battle-conscious, prepared to fight. Other interests may come and go (since no one can maintain a constant, conscious focus on the war), but always the thought lies just beneath the surface that there is a war to be fought and that we are about to win the big one that will bring it to an end. Mentally, such troops are prepared for battle; whereas mentally, the troops with low morale try desperately to forget the war and get out of it at any cost. Mentally, they may even try to deny its existence. Such a mentality leads to defeat.

What sort of mentality do you maintain? Are you perpetually conscious of the fact that the Lord has called you to fight for Him? Are you alert to the enemy's assaults? Are you anxious to rout him once again so that you can edge the war nearer to its end? In other words, soldier, how is *your* morale?

"Well," you say, "I hardly knew I was in the army until I began to read this book. And, as for battles, well... I certainly haven't been looking forward to them. I guess the belt of my mind is hanging pretty loose."

Then pull it tight and get ready for the next battle! Remember, it is now possible to win, since Christ has suffered and died for you. He has released you from the penalty and the dominion of sin by His atoning sacrifice. There is therefore no reason for you to lose and every reason for you to win. Take heart!

Remember the spies of Israel? With most of them God was displeased because they saw the enemy as giants and themselves as grasshoppers by comparison. They were dispirited and their report brought discouragement upon the entire people. Only Joshua and Caleb saw that the battle was the Lord's and that the Creator of the universe was surely capable of overcoming these puny giants (Numbers 13). But the majority report prevailed despite the great prospects offered by a land flowing with milk and honey.

Your influence may be the source of poor morale in your church, your family, and your children. Parents who are defeated in their battles with sin and who all but deny the reality of the war between the seeds do little to inspire courage and biblical daring in their children. No wonder so many of the children emerging from our Christian schools are weak, pampered, and both unable and unwilling to fight the flesh. By their lives and their words, defeated teachers and parents have dispirited the troops.

On the other hand, without bragging about your victories (those who are really victorious don't have to tell others), do you exude the joys of ever-prevailing progress against the enemy? Does your congregation take heart when they see you coming bloody but unbeaten from the battle, having once more routed the enemy? More important, what does God think?

I am not going to extend this chapter. Its short length is disproportionate to its importance. But I do want to emphasize the fact that one is really not armed at all if he is not "armed with this thought," as Peter puts it: that Christ has defeated the enemy and made it possible for his soldiers to do so too.

Unless you can see beyond your day-by-day battles to ultimate victory, when the Lord in grace will richly bless His faithful troops, you will lack the mindset necessary to wage war successfully. So maintain a military mentality! Tighten your belt in preparedness and in good morale! If Christ's death and His Word do not inspire you to preparedness and high morale, what will?

14

Deserters

Recently a woman told me how a number of young people had been affected adversely by the apostasy of a bright young leader. They had looked up to him, and when he repudiated the faith they were so shaken that they began questioning the reality of their own faith and of the Savior in whom they had placed their faith. Her words reminded me of Chuck Templeton's defection from the faith years ago, after he attended a liberal seminary for graduate work. He turned his back on his evangelistic ministry, then on his faith, and became a TV announcer in Canada instead. How do such things happen? What is going on, anyway? Why, nothing unusual at all. In every war there have been plenty of deserters.

A few months ago my wife and I were doing research in the National Archives, looking for the names of some soldiers who had served in the Confederate Army. We were surprised at the number of deserters in the records. Josephus, the famous historian of the Roman war against the Jews who describes the fall of Jerusalem, was a deserter to the Romans. As a result he was able to write about the war from both perspectives.

In his book *Your Kids and Mine,* Joe E. Brown tells a humorous story about an American taken prisoner by a German who knew English. The German was chewing on unspeakable gray ersatz rations that he could hardly eat. The American began describing what he had had that day for lunch. He even claimed that there would be steak for supper. Eventually, in order to get a decent meal, the German exchanged places with the American, whom he allowed to take him prisoner and escort him back to a meal. In telling the story to an officer, the American got to the part about the steak, admitting that he had exaggerated quite a bit to turn Spam into steak. But the captain said, "Do you know what we are having tonight?" "No," he answered. The reply was "steak."[1] Soldiers desert all the time, as you can see, for all sorts of reasons.

People Who Desert God

What is taking place when people desert the army of the Lord? Should we be shaken to the roots when someone we thought was a solid Christian goes over to the enemy? Is it possible for a real Christian ever to desert?

First, let's make it clear that when a trusted leader or close friend repudiates the Christian faith, there is no reason for other Christians to question their past commitment to the Lord. It is the *Lord Jesus Christ* who promised never to leave us or forsake us (and He has kept that promise). It is in *Him* that we have believed, and He has not failed us. If your faith is in someone else rather than the Lord, then of course you will have reason to doubt when the one in whom you have trusted caves in. But the Lord will never do so. Persons who are so badly shaken by the desertion of some leader or friend give evidence that their faith is at least in part wrongly placed. The desertion which rocks them to the foundations provides an opportunity for them to examine the object of their faith, and to place it properly in Jesus Christ for the future.

Those who leave the Lord and never return repentant were never with Him in the first place:

> They went out from us, but they weren't of us; because if they had been of us, they would have remained with us. But this happened that it might appear that they all aren't of us (1 John 2:19).

When the going gets tough, the war separates the true from the false. That is why a persecuted church is nearly always a more pure church than a tolerated one. In America today, because of the relatively easy course of life that a Christian may live, in some sections of the country it is even fashionable to be a Christian. That is a dangerous condition for the church. Too many tares, that look like wheat, grow up in the midst of the church. If persecution (and sometimes it takes only a little) arises, many of the tares leave the church on their own.

But note that John says two things with regard to those who desert. First, the reason they left is because they were really not of us in the first place. That is to say, they were never truly Christians. Like those mentioned in Hebrews who benefit from all the blessings of close association with Christians but eventually "fall away" (Hebrews 6:4-8), so too these professing Christians who eventually left John and the churches to which he was writing were never true Christians at all. For some reason (family pressure, financial gain, mere attraction to the lifestyle of Christians, interest in some possible marriage partner, or whatever) they professed to be Christians. At the time they may even have deceived themselves into believing they were. But when persecution arose, or the benefit which they hoped to realize failed to materialize, they left.

There is a second reason why John says they left. In the providence of God He wanted to reveal to the church that there are false members in it, and in particular who some of them were. So when some depart from the church, shaking the dust off their feet, rather than be appalled at the fact you should recognize that God is keeping you from becoming complacent about your faith. He is urging you to check its genuineness and warning you to keep a wary eye open for the false members mixed into your fellowship who can dilute its impact on the world and the flesh and turn it in wrong directions. In short, to see persons turn from Jesus Christ and repudiate His church is, in the providence of God, meant to be a blessing.

In a similar vein, Paul (who deplored divisions in the church and wrote the very epistle in which he said the words that follow) explained:

> I hear that divisions exist among you, and in part I believe it, because there must be factions among you so that it may appear who is approved among you (1 Corinthians 11:18,19).

Again, it is the ones who hang in there when others leave, and who continue to adhere to the truth and to the One who is the truth, who prove that their faith is genuine.

There is foxhole religion that manifests itself ultimately in apostasy, but there is also another reason for desertion:

Deserters Leave over the War Within

"What can you mean by that?" you ask. "After all, near the beginning of this book you said that unbelievers have no such war within because they are slaves to sin, are without the Spirit, and are incapable of fighting the flesh even if they desired to, which they do not (at least at any level of depth, though they may wish to escape from its consequences at times). So how does the war within drive them from Christ?"

That is a good question. Let's address it. When they come into the body of true believers, unbelievers enter an army that is at war with the one to whom the unbelievers swear allegiance. Therefore everything they see and hear is out of kilter. These people pray, they read their Bibles, and—preeminently—they are concerned about their lifestyle. Listening to preaching that emphasizes the need to defeat the enemy within and attending prayer meetings in which Christians plead for strength and wisdom to fight the battle successfully soon begins to chafe on the unbeliever. He recognizes that this is not his crowd. He sees no necessity to struggle with such matters. The whole business is foreign to him and at length grows repulsive. Some unbelievers, therefore, see no future for themselves there and wander off.

Perhaps nothing is more repugnant to an unbeliever than "these Christians who are always bewailing their sins. I don't see it; I think people aren't all that bad. And even if they are, it is certainly of no profit to agonize over failures the way they do." That is the way an unbeliever in the midst of Christian activity may begin to think. And his words, bitter and resentful over his disillusionment, may not describe any unbiblical concern about sin or any morose subjectivity growing out of self-centered introspection on the part of those Christians whose attitudes repulse him. The problem is in him, not in them. Of course at times Christians may fall into traps of subjectivity, self-centeredness, etc. But they don't have to do any such thing to turn off the unregenerate person in their midst. He is as uncomfortable as a fish out of water when he hears Christians speaking about the war within.

"I've been attending this Sunday school class for five weeks now, and all I've heard you talk about is sin, sin, sin. You're more concerned about this so-called 'sin' than you are about the political scene around you. I can't understand it. If you really want to lambaste sin, why not start with Congress? There's plenty of sin there in the way they steal our money and the graft that goes on. I don't know why you sit here, week after week, flagellating yourselves."

So spoke Bob, an unbeliever in the midst. He had not yet joined, and in time he left the class and the church because he would have nothing to do with "a bloody gospel that tells you how to get rid of sin," as he expressed it. "Sin, sin, that's all you ever talk about," were his parting words.

The war within, then, is not only an *unknown* experience to the unbeliever but it is the very point at which he sticks. Here, in the concerns and the actions of those around him in the church, the differences stand out. He recognizes that these are not his kind of people; these are not his concerns; this is not his kind of religion. Of course many unbelievers, like tares, grow to the end. But it is also true that many separate themselves long before that. They simply have a hard time understanding Christians (1 Corinthians 2:9-16) and soon discover that they do not particularly enjoy their company.

What shall we say then of deserters? They will always be with us, for the reasons already stated in this chapter. While you should try to win them to Christ, you must never become disconcerted by the fact that those who reject Him go over to the enemy. After all, they are simply returning to the camp to which they belong. That they should misunderstand the war within and speak disparagingly of your earnest efforts to win battles for your Lord should be expected. Did not unregenerate people also misunderstand and misrepresent the Lord Himself?

Your responsibility is to take your eyes off the deserters and focus them on your Lord. Don't let them trouble you. You never know the heart of another person. Outwardly he may for a time seem genuine, but time will tell. That is the message of the passages we have been studying. Of one thing you may be sure: No true believer will ultimately desert his Lord. He is kept by Jesus Christ Himself, so that not one of those whom the Father gave Him will be lost (John 17).

15

The Outcome

Death

Of course you can die—physically. Death came on all men because of Adam's sin, and "sin, when fully matured, brings forth death" (James 1:15; cf. Romans 5:12). James warns Christians that the ultimate outcome of the flesh's desire, unconquered, is death.

If you lose enough battles (or even one crucial battle) with the flesh, it could mean your death. The flesh can kill you! Think of the thousands of believers who, failing to win the battle with drunkenness, have died from poisoning their livers. Paul tells the Ephesian Christians not to get drunk with wine because, he says, drunkenness leads to "utter ruin" (Ephesians 5:18; the word translated "utter ruin" is literally "unsalvageableness").

Proverbs speaks plainly about the fool who turns in to the adulteress's house. He asks, "Can a man carry fire in his bosom and his clothes not be burned?" (Proverbs 6:27 Berkeley). He describes the time when he doesn't get away with it (6:29-35) and ends a series of vignettes along that theme by saying:

> Suddenly he goes after her, as an ox goes
> to the slaughter...till an arrow strikes his

> liver . . . he does not know it will cost his life
> (7:22,23 Berkeley).

The husband has caught him in the act—and killed him!

Then there is that difficult passage in 1 John 5:16:

> If anybody sees his brother committing a
> sin that doesn't lead to death, he shall ask
> and He will give life to him (that is, to those
> committing a sin that doesn't lead to death).
> There is a sin that leads to death; I don't say
> that you should make a request [or in-
> quiries] about that.*

Difficult as it may be, certain facts are clear. The first is that there are sins which Christians (note the word "brother") commit that lead to their deaths. Second, it is not for other Christians to search out all the facts (i.e., "to ask or inquire") about any such sin (gossip and idle curiosity are condemned). All he must do is pray.

What is this sin that leads to death? Well, it could be one of two things: either a sin that is punishable by death before the law (capital offenses of this sort are mentioned in Deuteronomy 21:22; 22:23,24) or a sin that, for His own good reasons, the Lord sees fit to punish with death (cf. 1 Corinthians 11:30). Either way, the sin leads to *physical* death.

---

* In this verse there are two distinct words for asking. The first, having to do with prayer, means "to ask *for* [something]"; the second, having to do so with inquiries, means "to ask *about* [something]."

Whenever death is the outcome of some sin, it is clear that death results from failure to win some battle, or battles, with the flesh.

So, if for no other reason than to avoid a premature death (Proverbs and 1 Corinthians 11 both appeal to this motive), you must learn to fight sin in your flesh. That is not the highest motive, of course, but it is one that everyone can understand; so God appeals to it. On the other hand, it is important to live out the fullness of your life for Christ. So, even desiring length of days can (and should) be part of the same higher motive.

Be careful not to confuse things that differ. Spurgeon once said:

> You are only a soldier in the king's army, and you may die in a ditch, but it does not matter what becomes of you as long as the King is exalted.[1]

That is true enough (though in the namby-pamby, pseudo-Christian milieus that exist all too widely today you won't hear such teaching), but it is not what I am talking about. Death is not martyrdom, but disobedient foolishness when you do yourself in by sin.

"Hard language," you say. Yes. But hard truth must be felt! "If the trumpet gives an indistinct sound, who will get ready for battle?" (1 Corinthians 14:8).

The Enemy's Defeat

As part of the Lord's army, engaged in the mopping-up expeditions that have followed the cross, you have been given the rare privilege of helping the Lord defeat His foe. After all, as I have been saying all through this book, ultimately the war within is not *your* battle. That is why it is not a personal feud of some kind. It is a part of the global and cosmic wars in which God is bringing down the hosts of Satan to their final doom. That's what makes the task so important. And that's why it is such a privilege for God to allow you to fight this battle with Him as a soldier in His armed forces.

Of course, God could wipe Satan out with a word. Indeed, there need not have been any war at all had not God for His own good reasons decreed it. Nor does God need you to fight His battles for Him. For some inscrutable reason God has planned to do things this way. And, as part of His plan, His people who fight in His cause will be caught up and included in His glorious victory. That will be the wondrous outcome for the faithful. Listen to some of the hints of the coming glory in which you shall participate:

> This is a clear indication of God's righteous judgment that you may be considered worthy of God's empire, for which indeed you are suffering, since it is just for God to repay affliction to those who are afflicting you, and give rest to you who are being afflicted (and to us) at the revelation of the Lord Jesus from the sky with His mighty angels.... They will pay the penalty of eternal ruin and separation from the presence of the Lord and from the glory of His might when He comes to be glorified by (or "in") His saints and to be admired by all

those who have believed (2 Thessalonians 1:5-10).

Therefore I endure for the sake of the chosen ones, so that they too may obtain the salvation that is in Christ Jesus, together with eternal glory.... "If we died with Him, we also shall live with Him; if we endure, we also shall reign with Him..." (2 Timothy 2:10-12).

Don't be surprised at the fiery ordeal that is coming upon you to test you, as though something strange were happening to you; rather, insofar as you share in Christ's sufferings, be glad, that at the revelation of His glory you may be very glad. If you are reproached because of Christ's name, you are happy, because the Spirit of glory and of God rests on you (1 Peter 4:12-14).

Now the God of all help, Who has called you to His eternal glory in Christ, after you have suffered a little, will equip, support, strengthen and firmly establish you (1 Peter 5:10).

And, finally:

This temporary light affliction is producing for us an eternal weight of glory that is beyond all comparison (2 Corinthians 4:17).

In all of these passages there is war and victory. God's own people, who suffer now, will reign with Him in glory. Because they have participated in His war for a time, they will forever participate in the spoils of His victory. That is the glorious outcome which all the true saints of God anticipate.

So the message of the Bible is that the enemy's defeat is your triumph with Jesus Christ. What a marvelous hope!

God's Honor

Most important of all is the fact that God will be honored. In the passages quoted above, surely you cannot miss the fact that it is *God's* glory and *God's* honor in which we bask. We are nothing by comparison, but are honored as an honor to Him. In that day, when He puts down all enemies, God will be all in all (1 Corinthians 15:24-28).

There is little more to say, but it is enough. No one can describe what that day will be like; the brightness of his coming at His revelation will be with such effulgence that doubtless we shall be speechless. We shall admire Him in wonder, revel in His glory, and stand astonished at it all. At last the war will be over, and we shall understand. The scars, the wounds, the suffering, the agony will all be seen to be worth it. We shall hear our Lord Himself say, "Well done." That will be enough![2]

Present Results

There are immediate outcomes of fighting the battles of the Lord, outcomes that we can begin to appreciate and realize right now, even before the final end of hostilities. I shall mention several of these.

First, fighting brings people close together. You will get to know other Christians better as you provide reinforcement for them and they for you. Most of all, you will begin to appreciate the presence of the Holy Spirit within you as you would not in any other way. You will experience His wisdom, His strength, and His encouragement as you call upon Him in the battle with the flesh and learn of His care and sufficiency for you.

You will grow as a person, learning from the trial of your faith to become more patient and long-suffering. You will build endurance and your faith will grow. All the virtues mentioned by James and Peter are the outcome of struggle (James 1:2-4; 2 Peter 1:3-8). War is always a time of opportunity as well as a time of testing. There are opportunities not only for those who fight well most of their lives, but opportunities for all the Brads and Mildreds who repent and grow—and opportunities for *you*.

You can learn from failure, as we have seen. You can learn from success—to honor God and not take the credit yourself. When you succeed, you must thank the One who enabled you to do so; when you fail, you must learn to take the blame.

You can learn from watching others as they fight. Their failures and their successes can be of great help to you in your battles with the flesh. You can also learn to reach out of yourself, praying for your suffering brothers and restoring those who fall beneath the onslaughts of the flesh.

And, finally, the greatest present outcome may be that you are driven by adversity to the Bible—to study it as you never would have otherwise, to apply it more seriously than you ever would have before, to appreciate its provisions as you never could have apart from affliction. That is what the psalmist discovered was the outcome of his afflictions:

> Before I was afflicted, I went astray; but now I keep Thy saying.... It is good for me that I was afflicted, so that I may learn Thy statutes (Psalm 119:67,71 Berkeley).

Properly fought, with recouping when there is failure, the war within can have only a good outcome. And of course in the day in which the battles have all been fought and final victory has been achieved, you will no longer fight. There will be no more war. God will have laid aside this body of yours, burying with it the "flesh" which so grievously afflicted you, and which is now so bitter an opponent. Or He will have immediately transformed that body into the glorious body that all the dead in Christ shall receive at the revelation of His glory: a body like His!

That is the outcome for you, Christian. Remember it during the difficult days that you will yet experience. Remember, and take heart. The fiery trials are but for a time. They will pass, and glory will come.

16

Conclusion

Some day in glory you will look back on the long, weary battle and cry, "The war is over!" How wonderful that will be!

That day has not yet arrived; it is not yet time to beat your swords into plowshares. Rather, listen to Joel:

> Declare a holy war; arouse your warriors.... Beat your plowshares into swords and your pruninghooks into spears (Joel 3:9,10 Berkeley).

There is still much work to be done, and perhaps much suffering to be endured. If this book has done nothing more, I hope it has alerted you to the fact that you live under wartime conditions, has revealed the glorious outcome in which you will participate, has shown you your part in the war, and has encouraged you to:

> lift your listless hands and strengthen your weak knees (Hebrews 12:12).

The writer of Hebrews is concerned about lethargy. He urges:

> Consider Him Who endured such opposition from sinners against Himself, so that

you won't get tired and give up—in your
struggle against sin you haven't yet had to
resist to the point of shedding your blood
(Hebrews 12:3,4).

Of course Christ did so. That's what the war is all
about: sin, and its final overthrow by the cross of
Christ!

Christian, how goes the war within? What must
you do after reading this book? Take heart in the
midst of suffering and pain? Well, there are plenty
of biblical promises quoted throughout the book
that can give you that encouragement. One reason I
set them out in block quotations, rather than running them into the text, is to make them easy to
locate. I urge you to go back and reread them. A
prime purpose of this book is to encourage faltering
Christians.

Perhaps you have failed terribly. You may be in
disgrace. You may see no way out of your dilemma.
Reread those chapters that tell you what God can do
for a Mildred or a Brad. Repent. Return to the
resources that God has provided for languishing
soldiers, and, if necessary, don't hesitate for another
moment to call for reinforcements. As a matter of
fact, it might be wise for you to get on the phone
right now. Don't allow the voices of the world to lure
you away from any good resolutions that may have
arisen from reading the promises of God. Forget
what all others are saying; turn from the influence
of friends in the world (who, when your money is
gone or your value to them is at an end will desert
you as surely as Rob left Mildred) and return to
Christ and His people. Go home to the Father's
house; that's where you belong.

Possibly you have been fighting well. Good; continue to grow. But remember that you are in a dangerous position. You have been giving the enemy a hard time. He is not going to take that lying down. He will make every effort to bring you down, along with him, to the grave if necessary. Take heed lest you fall. Give the Lord the glory for all you have been able to do. Thank Him for protecting and using you. Continue to call upon Him alone for wisdom and strength. Don't grow weary, especially when you see so many other Christians who are not pulling their share of the load. Rather, bear their burdens, by restoring them, so that they will once more be fit to fight alongside you.

Whatever your condition, soldier of the cross, remember that the Lord is with you and wants you to win. You *can* win and you *will* win if you fight in His strength. Life is not really all that long. In just a little while you will taste the fruits of ultimate victory, and then all the miseries of the present life—the battles, the wounds, the casualties on the field—will be but a sanctified memory in which you will praise the Lord that in His mercy He was willing to use you, with all your imperfections, to fight for Him.

Yes, that is all true—wonderfully so. But for now . . . do you hear the bugle sounding? The enemy is once again astir; the flesh is up and moving. Be alert; he is poised for the attack. Your God is calling you to the front. Put on your armor—all of it. Pick up your sword and go forth into battle—for Him.

NOTES

Chapter 1—Who Started It?

1. Robert S. Candlish, *The Book of Genesis* (Edinburgh, Adam and Charles Black, 1884), p. 60.
2. For a detailed discussion of the war throughout the entire Old Testament, see James R. Graham, *The Divine Unfolding of God's Plan of Redemption* (Grand Rapids: Zondervan, 1948).

Chapter 2—The War Within

1. Phillips Brooks, *Visions and Tasks* (New York: E.P. Dutton and Co., 1886), p. 269.

Chapter 4—What's the War Like?

1. Harry Blamires, *Where Do We Stand?* (Ann Arbor: Servant Books, 1980), p. 38.
2. For a detailed discussion of how most supposedly Christian education is pervasively pagan education rather than Christian, and what can be done about it, see my book *Back to the Blackboard* (Phillipsburg: Presbyterian and Reformed Publishing Co., 1982).
3. For more about discernment, see Jay E. Adams, *A Call to Discernment* (Eugene: Harvest House, 1987).

Chapter 6—The Enemy's Power

1. Charles H. Spurgeon, Compiled by Tom Carter, *Spurgeon at His Best* (Grand Rapids: Baker, 1988), p. 57.

Chapter 7—The Enemy Within

1. Phillips Brooks, *The Battle of Life* (New York: E.P. Dutton and Co., 1910), p. 82.
2. John Calvin, "On Enduring Persecution," in Jay E. Adams, ed., *Sermon Analysis* (Denver: Accent Books, 1986), p. 87.
3. Brooks, *Battle*, p. 83.
4. Leroy Nixon, ed., *Sermons on Job* (Grand Rapids: Baker), p. 241.
5. Steven Brown, *No More Mr. Nice Guy!* (Nashville: Nelson, 1986), p. 117.
6. For a view in many respects similar to the one set forth in this chapter, together with detailed exegesis, see Ronald K. Fung, "The Impotence of the Law," in W. Ward Gasque and Wm. Sanford LaSor, eds., *Scripture, Tradition, and Interpretation* (Grand Rapids: Wm. B. Eerdmans, 1978), pp. 34-48.

Chapter 8—Fighting with the Spirit's Sword

1. Jean Marie Barette, *The Clowns of God* (Toronto: Bautom, 1982), p. 320.
2. In James Hastings, *The Great Christian Doctrines: Prayer* (New York: Charles Scribner's Sons, 1919), p. 259.
3. Carter, *Spurgeon*, p. 320.

Chapter 9—The Believer's Other Weapons

1. William Hendriksen, *New Testament Commentary: Ephesians* (Grand Rapids: Baker, 1967), p. 280.
2. John Calvin, *Sermons on Timothy and Titus* (Edinburgh: Banner of Truth Trust, 1983), p. 866.
3. Carter, *Spurgeon*, p. 146.
4. Phillips Brooks, *Seeking Life* (New York: E.P. Dutton, 1910), p. 244.
5. Ibid., p. 242.

6. Ibid.
7. Calvin, "Persecution," p. 100.

Chapter 10—Calling In Reinforcements

1. For help on understanding and implementing this command, please see my book *Ready To Restore* (Phillipsburg: Presbyterian and Reformed Publishing Co., 1981).

Chapter 11—Defeat

1. Martin Luther, *Sermons*, Vol. 8—J.N. Lemker, trans. (Grand Rapids: Baker Book House, 1988), p. 156.
2. Ibid., p. 159.
3. Ibid., p. 169.
4. Ibid., p. 172.
5. For a thorough discussion of 2 Timothy 3:15-17, see my book *How to Help People Change* (Grand Rapids: Zondervan, 1986). The book is an exposition and application of these verses.
6. Phillips Brooks, *The Purpose and Use of Comfort* (New York: E.P. Dutton, 1910), pp. 364, 365.

Chapter 12—Hindrances

1. Luther, *Sermons*, p. 152.
2. Ibid., p. 275.

Chapter 14—Deserters

1. Joe E. Brown, *Your Kids and Mine* (Garden City: Doubleday, Doran and Co., Inc., 1944), pp. 166-69.

Chapter 15—The Outcome

1. Carter, *Spurgeon*, p. 310.
2. In Revelation chapters 2 and 3 we find Christ's sevenfold promise to soldiers who overcome (2:7,11,17,26; 3:5,12,21).

Other Titles by Dr. Jay Adams
available from your bookstore or
directly from TIMELESS TEXTS
1-800-814-1045

What to do on Thursday—A Layman's Guide to the Practical Use of the Scriptures
by Jay E. Adams   144pp. paperback

> The Bible has the answers, but can you find, understand and apply them?
> *What to do on Thursday* teaches you how to study and interpret your Bible
> to answer the questions that arise all week at work, at play, at home, and at
> school.

> Dr. Adams has written this study to prepare you to meet the challenges of
> this fast-moving world with decisions that will honor God. The practical use
> of the Scriptures on an everyday basis is crucial to all of God's people. You
> can't wait for your pastor to preach a sermon that applies to your need now.
> *What to do on Thursday* will help you prepare a template of priorities that
> will order your life in a Godly pattern.

The Grand Demonstration—A Biblical Study of the So-Called Problem of Evil
by Jay E. Adams   119pp. paperback

> Why is there sin, rape, disease, war, pain and death in a good God's world?
> Every Christian asks this question—but rarely receives an answer. Read this
> book and discover what God Himself says.

> *The Grand Demonstration* penetrates deeply into scriptural teaching regard-
> ing the nature of God. Moving into territory others fear to tread, Dr. Adams
> maintains that a fearless acceptance of biblical truth solves the so-called
> "problem of evil".

Teaching to Observe—The Counselor as Teacher
by Jay E. Adams   131pp. paperback

> Here is a book that is long overdue. Carl Rogers convinced a generation of
> counselors to listen and reflect while insisting that teaching is taboo.
> Though Rogerianism failed, and is now largely passé, many counselors still
> hesitate to teach their counselees.

> Dr. Adams shows not only that God obligates Christian counselors to teach,
> but how they may do so in ways that will help counselees both learn and
> "observe" those things that Christ "commanded" according to Matthew
> 28:20. He demonstrates clearly, using illustrations to which you will reso-
> nate, that effective biblical counseling requires teaching. This book, the only
> one of its kind, is must reading for every serious Christian.

A Thirst For Wholeness
by Jay E. Adams   143pp. paperback

> How healthy is your spiritual integrity? Do your actions speak so loudly that
> people won't listen? *A Thirst for Wholeness* provides the solution to this
> common problem. Drawing on the book of James, Dr. Adams concentrates
> on how you can become a complete Christian from the inside out. As you
> study the inner dynamics involved in this process, you'll learn how to get
> your spiritual beliefs and your everyday actions in sync.

Truth Applied—Application in Preaching
by Jay E. Adams   144pp. paperback

> Too often, a sermon founders on a preacher's failure to make a good connec-
> tion between a message originally delivered to God's people millennia ago
> and the congregation in the here and now. Dr. Adams has long been con-
> cerned for the art and science and passion of preaching. In this book he
> offers a cogent, biblical philosophy of application, together with practical
> suggestions about how the busy preacher can readily implement it.

The Christian Counselor's Commentary Series
by Jay E. Adams   all volumes hardback

Vol. 1—I & II Corinthians
Vol. 2—Galatians, Ephesians, Colossians & Philemon
Vol. 3—I & II Timothy and Titus
Vol. 4—Romans, Philippians, and I & II Thessalonians

> This series of commentaries is written in everyday English. A must for the
> layman as well as the Pastor/Counselor. Dr. Adams' everyman style of com-
> munication brings forth these biblical truths in a clear understandable way
> that typifies his writings. He does not try to duplicate the standard, more
> technical types of commentaries but supplements them with the implications
> of the text for God-honoring counseling and Christian living.

The Christian Counselor's New Testament
translated by Jay E. Adams   leather & synthetic bindings

> A special translation by Dr. Adams with extensive footnotes and topical side
> columns. This Bible was specially designed to help the Christian in study as
> well as counseling. *The Christian Counselor's New Testament* is very user
> friendly. It leads you through those tough counseling topics by using the
> Margin Notations and Notation Index for the topic or related topics. Easily
> used during the counseling session.